T0334237

Group Coaching for Women Leaders

This book is an invaluable resource for those looking to lead high-functioning women groups, and a testament to the power of group coaching for women leaders.

Dr. Hélène Seiler advocates for the expansion of group coaching to support the fulfilment of women leaders, providing a comprehensive review of the relevant academic literature on group coaching for women leaders and an in-depth analysis of her reflective notes over the last 15 years. This book shares the author's experience as an international group coach and an executive coach for women leaders, and echoes the voices of her former group members. Using case studies and practical tips, the author offers recommendations when forming a new collective of women leaders, shares best practices in high-functioning groups, provides solutions when dealing with breakdowns within a group, and provides guidelines to lead change when a group composition evolves. This book also addresses the potential impact of technology and artificial intelligence on the stakeholders of group coaching. Each chapter contains key points, multi-cultural case studies, and ends with reflective questions to enrich and personalize the reader's learning experience.

Group Coaching for Women Leaders is an essential resource for group coaches working with women leaders internationally, for academic leaders looking to extend their offerings for student coaches, and for corporate sponsors interested in augmenting the power of women leadership development initiatives in their organizations.

Hélène Seiler is an executive coaching practitioner and adjunct faculty with 25 years of experience in North America, Western Europe, and Asia. She holds a Doctorate in coaching and mentoring from Oxford Brookes University, UK, and has attained over 15,000 hours of private practice delivering individual and group coaching engagements for senior management in international organizations, in the not-for-profit and for-profit sectors.

Group Coaching for Women Leaders

Belonging and Thriving Through Collective Leadership Development

Hélène Seiler

Routledge
Taylor & Francis Group

NEW YORK AND LONDON

Designed cover image: © Getty Images

First published 2025
by Routledge
605 Third Avenue, New York, NY 10158

and by Routledge
4 Park Square, Milton Park, Abingdon, Oxon, OX14 4RN

Routledge is an imprint of the Taylor & Francis Group, an informa business

ISBN: 978-1-032-73302-9 (hbk)
ISBN: 978-1-032-72324-2 (pbk)
ISBN: 978-1-003-46519-5 (ebk)

DOI: 10.4324/9781003465195

Typeset in Times New Roman
by SPi Technologies India Pvt Ltd (Straive)

Contents

Group Coaching for Women Leaders

About this Book

I started my journey as a group coaching practitioner 15 years ago in Southeast Asia. My business partner and I were designing a women leadership development program for the Asia Pacific Region of an international organization. Our corporate clients were concerned with the continued weakness of their women leadership pipeline and the small percentage of women at the top of their organization. They recognized that women's specific leadership development opportunities and challenges were not sufficiently addressed within in their current portfolio of mixed-gender leadership development initiatives. We agreed with them that leadership development theory and practice were still largely developed by men for men. We were aligned in our thinking that leadership development was still anchored in traditional patriarchal models, with little regards for women's specific challenges and opportunities.

As we co-designed the program, we suggested to dedicate a full day to a leadership development activity that would not only address women leaders' unique challenges, but would also build on their strengths such as connectedness and collaboration. At the time, group coaching lacked theorization and was still a rarely used intervention. We powered through, leaning on our complementary experience and on the limited literature that was available at the time. Our reflections lead to the design of a one-day experience of group coaching on the last of a five-day women leadership development program. We discovered that by using a very simple model of appreciative inquiry, each member would receive powerful insights through the facilitated support of their peers. This women leadership development program became a staple in the organization for the years to come.

Fast forward to 2024. Amazingly, little has changed since 2009.

Last year, while equal gender representation in corporate leadership featured as a key Corporate Social Responsibility initiative in the Women's Empowerment Principles,[1] women leaders represented only 20% of executive teams. While progress has been made over the last 15 years, there is little

DOI: 10.4324/9781003465195-1

hope for an increase in participation ten years from now.[2] Moreover, women continue to receive less hours of dedicated leadership development support overall than men, including, most critically, developmental feedback. They are less likely than men to secure a sponsor (a senior executive in their organization who actively supports their career progression) and less likely to be satisfied from their mentoring experience. In addition, they still express less satisfaction than men from mixed-gender leadership development initiatives. Arguably, less than a third of corporations offered leadership development programs focused on women leaders.

Group coaching continues to be an afterthought in most leadership development programs, perhaps understandably so. Indeed, there is still a lack of evidence explaining how group coaching works. Tellingly, the International Coaches Federation has so far neglected to develop a competency model for group coaches. As is often the case with an intervention that is still in a maturing stage, there is scarce theoretical research and little agreement on how to exactly define the process.

What is group coaching?

Group coaching is the facilitation of a voluntary, mutually beneficial coaching relationship between unaffiliated peers with shared interests, in service of the self-directed learning of each individual group member. For the women leaders I have had the privilege to work with all over the world, group coaching has provided a safe environment to belong and to thrive. Regular participation in group coaching offers not only long-lasting friendships, but also an opportunity to be heard, a chance to apprehend common and unique individual and social experiences, a platform to generate powerful insights, to define and experiment with new mindsets and behaviors, and to reflect on their outcomes in a supportive environment.

What to expect?

With this book, my intention is to equip group coaching practitioners, educators, and corporate commissioners with evidence that group coaching is an effective leadership development intervention for women leaders. The evidence is anchored in the first comprehensive review of the relevant academic literature on group coaching, complemented by an in-depth analysis of the reflective notes that I have relied on to develop as a group coach over the last 15 years.

This book offers six chapters that can be read independently depending on your needs. Each chapter is structured in the same manner. It starts with a summary of key points that orients you to the content of the chapter, continues with a development of these key points enriched with tables, visuals, and multi-cultural examples, and ends with reflective questions to personalize your learning experience.

Chapter 1 is dedicated to a review of the existing academic literature that is relevant to group coaching for women leaders. Readers will gain a greater understanding of the theories that underpin the practice and the differences between group coaching and other group interventions. In addition, the chapter highlights which group coaching practices are currently evidenced by research. Finally, I offer a review of the applications and value proposition of group coaching as documented in research.

Chapter 2 focuses on the experience of women leaders from the start to the end of the group coaching journey. It begins with a description of the different shapes a group coaching journey can take. Subsequently, I review the hopes and expectations of the members, the perceived benefits of group coaching overtime, the most frequent topics that women leaders bring to group coaching, and the key reasons why they wish to leave a group.

Chapter 3 turns its attention to the group coaching practitioner. I review the reflexions and actions of the group coach that support the forming of a group of women leaders. The chapter covers curation, ground rules, building cohesion, and psychological safety, as well as other tips and techniques to form a group.

Chapter 4 discusses how to activate the group to support the generation of new insights for each member. In the first section of the chapter, I review techniques that allow creative reflection in group coaching. In the second section of the chapter, I consider techniques that facilitate the transformation of these connections into applied learning. Finally, I discuss the implementation of evidence-based approaches and models to group coaching.

Chapter 5 focuses on the breakdowns that inevitably happen during the life of a group. I examine the different situations that can impact a group's journey and how the coach can address them. I cover ruptures of cohesion, difficult individual behaviours, problems of communication within the group, difficult group behaviors, and problematic behaviors from the group coach.

Chapter 6 addresses two fundamental emerging developments in group coaching and proposes future topics for research. The first topic is the much overdue need to design of a capacity model for the group coach. The second topic is the emergence of artificial intelligence in group coaching and what this means for the future of the discipline.

I hope this book will inspire you to start or expand your group coaching practice, to advocate for the use of group coaching as a key women leadership development intervention, or to promote the development of specific trainings and accreditations for its practitioners.

Notes

1 A partnership of UN Women and the UN Global Compact.
2 Current surveys indicate that, because progress with gender parity has been reversing at the middle management level since Covid, the pipeline of women leaders is currently decreasing.

Bibliography

Hideg, I., & Shen, W. (2019). Why still so few? A theoretical model of the role of benevolent sexism and career support in the continued underrepresentation of women in leadership positions. *Journal of Leadership & Organizational Studies*, *26*(3), 287–303.

Maher, N., & Hastings, R. (2023). Coaching for gender diversity: A thematic analysis of approaches, frameworks, and their efficacy. *Consulting Psychology Journal*, *75*(2), 154.

Why Diversity Matters Even More by McKinsey November 2023 Copyright © McKinsey & Company

Chapter 1

What We Know about Group Coaching for Women Leaders

Key points of Chapter 1

✓ Group coaching is a facilitated group process that supports the learning of individuals.

✓ When coaching a group of women leaders, the practitioner should consider how positivist, pragmatist and post-modernist theories of organizational feminism will inform their approach.

✓ While there is no theorization of group coaching, practice can be guided by the theories validated in its related disciplines, including group dynamics, facilitation, executive coaching, peer coaching, communities of practice, group therapy, group supervision, and group therapy.

✓ Group coaching is a versatile intervention that can be used on its own or as a module within a leadership development program. It addresses the needs of diverse leadership populations, provides healing, and supports both cognitive and behavioral change through a communal approach to learning.

✓ The conditions of success in group coaching are still understudied. Group cohesion sits at its foundation.

✓ Based on the research conducted on women's groups, it appears that leadership strengths that have been traditionally viewed as feminine are strongly associated with those needed to build and sustain group cohesion.

DOI: 10.4324/9781003465195-2

Purpose of Chapter 1

"Effective practice requires more than learning new tools, tips, and techniques. It must also include an exploration of the theories and values which underpin it". Thomas and Thorpe (2019), in their review of the literature of group facilitation, encourage the effective practitioner to develop a strong theoretical anchor. From their chosen theoretical perspective, the practitioner must examine the evidence that has been collected about the effectiveness of the tips, tools, and techniques that are offered to them. In the absence of enough evidence, they pause and reflect on the opportunity to experiment with them without causing unintended harm.

The purpose of Chapter 1 is to review the body of knowledge that has informed the practice of group coaching for women leaders. I will cover three theoretical domains: organizational feminism, group coaching, and women groups. I will then discuss the applications and benefits of group coaching as evidenced in the literature, followed by a review of the conditions that need to be in place to achieve these benefits. Finally, I will discuss situations when group coaching may not be the best intervention to support the leadership development of women leaders.

A working definition of group coaching

There is still confusion about the concept that group coaching represents. For some it evokes an intervention where members take turns receiving coaching from another member (with or without the support of the group leader) while other members observe and potentially give feedback afterwards. For others, it is a facilitated conversation about a common topic of interest, followed, possibly, by a consensus building exercise, or a call for collective action. In between these two views, variations abound.

In this book, as presented in the introduction, I narrowly define **group coaching** as **the facilitation of a collective coaching process provided by a group of unaffiliated peers with shared interests in service of the self-directed learning of each individual group member**. In other words, in group coaching, the group coaches each member one after the other while the group coach facilitates the process.

Group coaching is NOT team coaching. While scholars rightly argue that a team is a group, group coaching and team coaching have a different structure and purpose.

In group coaching:

* the focus is on individual learning for each member of the group
* relationships between group members are horizontal. They are not pre-defined and depend on a group coaching agreement between members

- the group is composed of members who have common interests. They have reached a similar level in their respective organizations and can relate to each other's opportunities and challenges
- the group members do not know each other when they join the group

In team coaching:

- the focus is on shared goals for a team. It might include individual team members' objectives if they are in service of the team's goals
- relationships between the team members are pre-defined by their respective roles within their organization
- the group is composed of team members who work together, know each other, and have a history in their working relationships
- most likely, team members will operate at different hierarchical levels

Theories of organizational feminism

Women are as ambitious as men. But they must work harder than men to prove that they are excellent leaders. Because women leaders are expected to be more nurturing and less assertive than men, they must navigate a double bind. When they choose to display leadership traits that are traditionally attributed to men, this must be achieved without violating gender norms. For instance, they will be expected to tone down a disagreement to avoid being unlikeable or seeming difficult.

The work environment was designed for a man whose only responsibility is to provide for his loved ones through paid work. In 2022, 70% of high-earning men in the USA had a stay-at-home partner. In these settings life-work integration is not supported. Women leaders are still predominantly in charge of the housework and childcare, throughout their career, even if they are the highest earner and even when 22% of high-earning women have a stay-at-home partner or spouse. To succeed in this environment, they have learned to accept it and conform, even if it means giving up part of their identity. They have focused on extreme agency, delegation in all compartments of their lives, constant self-improvement, and a seemingly infinite supply of energy and courage.

Amazingly, for the current generation of women leaders, it has felt more achievable to adjust to these gendered barriers than to challenge gendered assumptions and practices in organizations. Even though women spend more time than men to foster diversity, equity, and inclusion initiatives, results are slow to come. Arguably, cultural change is very difficult when the majority of those in power do not see the benefits of it. Hard pressure needs to be applied, and for a very long time for change to happen.

With the advent of MeToo, the denunciation of toxic male behaviors in the workplace has become more prevalent. However, little has happened to encourage men to embrace traits such as deference, humility, or cooperation that are more prevalent in women.

Under pressure from the Millennial generation, and because of the Covid pandemic, companies have extended flexible work arrangements. However, there continues to be an assumption from higher management (which is 80% men) that physical presence at the office leads to more reliability, team-orientation, and visibility. In addition, career interruptions or decelerations continue to hurt women's more than men's career progression.

Promotion criteria continue to favor men over women. Due to the persistence of bias, men tend to be promoted for their potential while women tend to be promoted for their past accomplishments. As a result, for every 100 men promoted to manager, 87 women are promoted.

In this context, feminist organizational theorists explore the intersection of gender and leadership theories in the workplace. While their roots are firmly grounded in feminist thinking, they have so far focused their research efforts on the equal access of women to positions of leadership.

Noting that leadership theory is founded in the heterosexual Western White man experience, feminist organizational theorists have developed over the last 25 years a rich body of theoretical and empirical knowledge about the women leadership experience. For example, empirical research on the glass ceiling has surfaced how corporate cultural norms and work practices reinforce social structures that disadvantage women. Benevolent sexism, a belief that women need to nurture their strengths outside of organizational leadership, is still implicit in many workplace settings. It continues to drive a pushback to gender equity at home and to gender inclusion at work. It explains the difficulties that women continue to face in getting the social support they need to integrate their personal and professional purposes.

Women leadership theorists agree about the challenges facing women in the workplace. However, they debate about ways these challenges can be addressed.

Acker's theoretical research on gender discrimination in the workplace, published in 1990, challenged the belief that organizations are gender neutral. Instead, the research posits that the workplace is defined by masculine principles, which negatively impacts women in their career. Twenty years later, Wharton expanded on Acker's work. Adopting a sociological perspective, she identified three frames to examine women leadership challenges in the workplace.

The first frame is individualist and views gender as a set of personal characteristics that can be changed as needed. The second frame envisions gender relationships in the workplace. Finally, the third frame concerns the status of women in society.

Positivist feminists (also called post-feminists in the literature) suggest that women operate within the first frame, focusing on improving the leadership skills that will help them thrive in their corporate and social systems. Pragmatist feminists tend to favor the second frame to influence corporate and societal norms from the inside out. Social constructivist feminists prefer the third frame and preconize a fundamental change in social structures and the toppling corporate cultural norms and practices from the outside in.

The question of intersectionality has emerged more recently in the theoretical organizational feminist literature. From this perspective women whose identity is also defined by other important characteristics such as being non-White, LGBTQ+, or over 50 (just to name a few) face cumulative challenges.

The positivist paradigm in women leadership research and practice

The positivist perspective views leadership excellence as a universal ideal. Consequently, it adopts a gender-neutral view of the workplace. This perspective, which has inspired the first wave of women leadership development programs, suggest that women operate in the first frame by "fixing themselves" so that they be promoted and lead effectively within the current corporate cultural norm.

Positivists endorse corporate competency models that promote manly strengths such as decisiveness, risk-taking, and competitiveness. They take it for granted that organizations have been designed to fit men's traditional life scripts. They do not challenge the consequences of this which include long hours, continuous employment from graduation through retirement, frequent relocation, crisis-oriented, and chaotic work patterns. Within this paradigm women are invited to follow these competency models if they want to be perceived as a leader. They are encouraged to view themselves as independent, and self-reliant. They are advised to improve self-esteem, self-confidence, self-control, courage, assertiveness, and networking. Women who conform to what has been called the "ideal worker" norm should expect to be invited to actively participate in the corporate ecosystem. Women who hold both family and work responsibilities must navigate a career that is linear and cumulative, which requires an uninterrupted life course at work during a prescribed period of their life.

The positivist perspective invites women to be self-aware of to the double bind effect, in which social expectations for women (be nice, hardworking, modest, nurturing, and collaborative) clash with perceived best practices in leadership (be bold, decisive, competitive, decisive, and assertive). The double bind effect marginalizes women who choose to lead using agentic leadership behaviors that are traditionally attributed to men. According to the role congruity theory, women are likely to suffer backlash for violating the prescriptive stereotype of being nurturing and communal. For example, they are likely to be ignored, interrupted, not given credit for their ideas, or passed over for jobs that involve taking charge. They will be labelled aggressive if they display assertive traits.

Women are therefore invited to skilfully navigate this paradox, toning down traits traditionally viewed as feminine to avoid losing credibility in the workplace while also toning down traits that are viewed as too masculine to avoid the backlash. This involves self-awareness and self-transformation, with an emphasis on self-confidence, self-efficacy, and authenticity, as well as the activation of powerful networking skills for support. Such efforts help women to internalize that they are solely responsible for their success with little acknowledgment of the structural barriers that they face.

However, research is lacking on the impact of the self-improvement imperative imposed on women. In fact, critics wonder whether this approach leads women to purposely repress some of their transformational leadership strengths, including inspirational motivation, intellectual stimulation, or individualized consideration, leading to less effective organizations. In addition, critics believe that these imperatives might negatively affect the construction and sustainability of women leadership identity, to the detriment of organizations, families, and the society at large.

Another adverse consequence of the positivist approach is a preference for the hiring of women leaders in crisis situations, on the assumption that they perform better than men nurturing key talent, taking the responsibility for the company's performance, and modelling hard-working habits. Unfortunately, such beliefs have not been evidenced in research: women leaders fail no less than men in crisis situations. This fallacy leads instead to more women leader burnout and disappearance from the leadership pool.

The pragmatist perspective in women leadership

The pragmatist perspective has influenced the development of a second wave of women leadership programs, where participants reflect on the critical factors for their career success and on how to further build on their strengths.

This perspective embraces empirical studies showing that the leadership traits that are more prevalent in women leaders are generally more effective to drive sustainable growth and stakeholder value. For example, research shows that communal characteristics most likely to be displayed by women are important for effective leadership. Women and men are encouraged to lean on strengths that are more likely to be described as feminine, including relationship building, inspiration, motivation, and collaboration. Pragmatists also recognize that the deployment of leadership traits is situational. Agentic, daring, ambitious and dominant approaches are sometimes needed.

As a result, both women and men leaders are invited to develop an eclectic approach to leadership, while leveraging their strengths authentically. Women and men are encouraged to collaborate and transform leadership models so that they can be more inclusive of a full range of leadership traits.

The pragmatist perspective is concerned with the feminist project and the replacement of the patriarchal social structures with inclusive social structures. Corporate mentoring and sponsoring programs promote and support women who take on impactful work assignments, obtain leadership positions, and gain visibility and power to drive incremental change from within. Because of its emphasis on studying effective organizational practices, the pragmatist perspective has significantly enriched the business case for more women leaders in organizations. Arguably, while an all-men team will make a better decision than an individual 57% of the time, a gender-diverse team will be more effective 73% of the time.

However, the pragmatic perspective offers precious few short-term solutions to address the burden of women who continue to cumulate work and family responsibilities. A case in point is the recent Covid pandemic. Corporations relied heavily on women leaders' interpersonal strengths which were perceived to be more effective in times of crisis. At the same time, societal expectations continued to dictate that they take on the bulk of caring duties for their loved ones outside of work. Arguably pragmatic feminist theorists fail to propose a concrete approach to design a work environment that is truly inclusive and reduces stress for their women employees.

As a result, women leaders must meet all these expectations in an environment that is unchanged. Of course, they can't do it all, and rely on a strong support system of paid help. This is another area where the pragmatic perspective fails to recognize that when women leaders strive to lessen the workload at home and at work, this is often achieved at the expense of less privileged women who assume such roles as caretakers, housekeepers, or administrators.

The view of constructivist feminists

The constructivist perspective offered by critical feminists emerged from the women's liberation movements in the late 1960s. They view gender as a social construction for the purpose of maintaining patriarchy and oppressing women.

They advocate for alternative organizational structures that reflect feminist values of equality, community, and participation. They do not believe that individual initiative can sufficiently challenge norms as advocated by pragmatists. Instead, they invite women leaders (and the men who follow them) to collectively lobby and advocate for profound structural and cultural changes in society outside of their respective organizations. MeToo is a good example of such call for change.

The constructivist view has also inspired younger generations to advocate for more inclusivity in the workplace, improved work life balance, career breaks, and more support for mental and physical healthcare.

In the United States primarily, constructivism has inspired the theorization of intersectionality that describes the lived experience of those who identify with two or more underrepresented social identities. Some intersectional groups have been formed to provide a safe space for members. Women's groups have been challenged to deepen their inclusive practice to allow for the emergence of intersectional voices and cross-fertilization.

A persistent critique of the constructivist perspective is that it devalues the first level of individual agency. It may prevent some women leaders from examining how their own individual beliefs and self-imposed barriers may work against them in their career.

In addition, it also places undue pressure on women and especially intersectional women to be the primary agents of societal and corporate change. For instance, women (and especially intersectional women) are often expected to take on more mentoring work, to spearhead employee resource groups, or to lead Diversity, Inclusion and Equity initiatives. When these efforts fail, the blame is placed on them: their reputation, career, and visibility might suffer as a result.

A theorization of group coaching

The practice of group coaching first emerged as a cost-effective process to support the professional development of educators and nurses. It lacks a body of theoretical and empirical research. Arguably it lags 20 years behind that of executive coaching.

In this section I approach the theorization of group coaching through that of its root disciplines, namely group theory, group facilitation, dyadic executive coaching, communities of practice, and group therapy. These disciplines share with group coaching common foundational theories including group dynamics, systems thinking, decision making, participative management, conflict management, mediation, cross cultural leadership, and collaborative learning.

Group theory

Group theory research is anchored in the study of group dynamics which started in the 1930s. Over the following decades the group was theorized as a social system. Research in group dynamic focused on the study of individual behaviors. In addition, stages of groups and communication patterns were described and explained. Most recently, the group is described as a complex adaptive system.

Two concepts from systems theory are important in group coaching practice: emergence and equifinality. Emergence means that a unique group spirit emerges from the interactions between group members. Equifinality means that each group may reach equifinal outcomes while implementing unique ways of proceeding. As a result, the group coach must be a student of group dynamics and co-create the process rather than prescribe it.

Group facilitation theory

Group level interventions have been an integral part of organizational development practices since the 1950s. Facilitation, similarly to team coaching, is firmly anchored in the theory of organizational learning, a meta-theory that explains how members of an organization interact to construct meaning and knowledge about the impact of organizational decisions, independently of individual tenures.

As a result, the purpose of group facilitation is consensus and group problem solving. The facilitator is tasked with organizing the process, including process design and group interaction techniques that enable psychological safety and personal responsibility. The facilitator is detached from the content and does not directly involve themselves in the substantive discussion. Often, the outcome of a facilitation is to achieve a short term, actionable goal so that the entire group can complete a task.

In contrast, the group coach activates the group so that each member feels supported to reflect on a personally relevant topic or to achieve a goal. The group coach empowers the group to co-create with them the thinking container and to activate the group dynamic. They invite each member to deploy coaching techniques such as active listening of open-ended questioning. They encourage members to stay away from evaluation and competitiveness. At times, the group coach can be an active part in the dialog and actively collaborate with group members to model the way and enhance the process. Organization learning theory has strongly influenced collaborative learning theory, including the conceptualization of single loop, double loop, and triple loop learning which the group coach can activate to address potential dysfunctions in the group (see Chapter 5).

Arguably, the group coach moves along a continuum between facilitation and education skills based on the needs of the group's participants, at times blurring boundaries, as shown in Table 1.1 below.

Executive coaching theory

Dyadic executive coaching is a dialogue between one client and one coach. There is increasing consensus in the community of researchers and practitioners of executive coaching that its purpose is individual learning, which

Table 1.1 The group coach in the continuum between facilitation and education

Facilitator	Group coach	Educator
Purpose is consensus and group problem solving	Purpose is individual learning	Purpose is individual learning
Content is decided by the group	Content is decided by the group	Content is decided by the organization and the educator
Organizes a process	Surfaces learning objectives	Teaches new concepts and skills
Creates and manages a thinking container	Elevates relationship building, insight generation and accountability skills to the group	Passes on knowledge
Manages group dynamics		Higher status
Detached from the content		Steers the group to apply the content taught
	Active member who at times will take part in the dialogue	Structured agenda
Often a short-term group outcome	Mix of short-term and long-term individual outcomes	Often a long-term individual outcome

is achieved through goal setting, active experimentation, and reflective practice. The process and the content of the intervention are co-created between the coach and the client, which can only be achieved through a trusting working relationship. The coach elevates relationship building, insight generation and accountability skills to support the client with their learning process. Theories of executive coaching derive from multiple disciplines, including psychotherapy, adult learning, leadership, adult development, transformational learning, relationship, organizations & systems, neuroscience, education, motivational interviewing, sports coaching, philosophy, meta-communication, narrative, psychodynamics, transpersonal and positive psychology. The International Coach Federation follows an expertise theory when credentialing coaches. It consists in researching, documenting, and recommending core competencies that need to be deployed to be certified as a coach. Some coaching schools espouse an evidence-based theory, committing to only use models whose effectiveness has been evidenced by scientific research. In other schools, the focus is on the capacity development of the coach to enable the successful deployment of competencies. The dimensions of the coach capacity include their personal qualities, ethical maturity, and leadership presence. A major ingredient that exists in group coaching and is not available in dyadic executive coaching is the group effect, which emerges from the contributions of members who offer multiple perspectives.

Dyadic peer coaching in practice

The practice of using coaching techniques for mutual peer support development emerged in the 1980s. Dyadic peer coaching suffers from a lack of theoretical research. As a result, its process has been conceptualized directly from executive coaching, with a narrower focus on skill development and goal achievement. As I indicated at the start of the chapter, some practitioners describe group coaching as the facilitation of dyadic peer coaching segments which are subsequently reviewed by the other group members, who act as observers. This technique is relevant when group members are taught coaching techniques. But this is not the definition of group coaching proposed in this book.

Communities of practice and executive peer advisory groups

The main purpose of communities of practice is to bring together peers who have common interests and no power differential. It emphasizes situated learning as a social process. The intent is to collectively explore the participants' respective practice, to surface areas for development and to support one another to set and achieve individual goals. The sharing of knowledge, experiences, and best practices is often the key method used. Communities of practice are not always facilitated.

Communities of practice for leaders started in the mid-fifties through the development of executive peer advisory groups. Examples include organizations offering curated groups worldwide such as the Young President's Organization, Vistage, and the Entrepreneur's Organization.

Group coaching has inherited the communities of practice's key principles of voluntarism, equal opportunity to participate, non-evaluation, non-competitiveness, and mutuality of support. The main difference with communities of practice is that the group coach invites its members to use less direct advice, and more open-ended questions. In addition, group coaching is focused on leadership learning rather than on technical or functional learning.

Group supervision

When a community of practice is facilitated, it may evolve as a supervision group. Group supervision has a long tradition in medical disciplines such as nursing. It is rapidly developing in executive coaching. In this format the group supervisor holds five key responsibilities: creating group norms that provide psychological safety, encouraging constructive feedback between practitioners, inviting them to discuss problematic feelings emerging from their practice, giving advice, soliciting advice from other practitioners, using various interactive teaching techniques, and monitoring practitioners' interaction.

In group supervision as in communities of practice, while each practitioner becomes the recipient of various sources of advice (including that of the supervisor), there is no pressure to signal agreement. Each participant is welcome to use or not use the input received based on their beliefs about what they need.

The group coach can rely on group supervision practice to enable effective contracting, mutual aid, and to encourage coaching behaviors. However, the group coach stays away from advising and invites group members to do the same, preferring informing approaches such as storytelling.

Group psychotherapy theory

Exactly like group coaching, group psychotherapy uses group dynamics to achieve each member's individual outcomes. The importance of the group psychotherapy literature for the group coach cannot be understated. Because its practice emerged decades ago, a large body of research has explored and explained its key benefits, many of which are applicable to group coaching. Group psychotherapy theory explains how universal human needs such as belonging, universality, hope, altruism, and meaning may be activated to anchor the process. In addition, group psychotherapy research has shown that group interventions create learning for the participants from both seeking and providing help.

Group psychotherapy research is particularly useful to better understand how cohesion drives the success of group intervention and holds important lessons for the group coach. Cohesion as a concept covers both the nature and the quality of the multiple types of relationships that develop in a group.

Vertical cohesion represents the relationships between each individual member and the leader. Horizontal cohesion represents both member-to-member and member-to-group relationships.

Qualitatively, cohesion is defined as the level of trust, bonding, and agreement that exist in the different categories of relationship.

Vertical cohesion in a group can be compared to the client-coach relationship in dyadic coaching (also called working alliance). In dyadic psychotherapy or coaching, it is one of the most important factors to the success of an intervention. However, meta-analyses in group therapy clearly demonstrate that vertical cohesion is the smallest contributor of group outcome. Both types of horizontal relationships are more effective. Arguably, the impact of cohesion is the strongest when the group leader puts emphasis on member-to-member interactions and supports a positive group climate.

A crucial difference in group psychotherapy is that participants goals are focused on stabilization and reducing clinical symptoms which prevent progress. For example, they will explore causes of resistance and be offered techniques to overcome them. In contrast, in group coaching, the group coach is assumed to work with participants whose clinical issues (if they have any) are treated elsewhere and are not an obstacle to growth. Group coaching supports members as they reflect on ways to augment their capacity. While the process may involve temporary destabilization, it is focused on enhancement.

Theories of women groups

The first mention of women groups appears in the mid-nineteenth century amongst suffragettes. Since then, women groups have been active on all continents, advocating for women's rights, promoting women's education, health, and leadership, supporting women's solidarity and empowerment, and challenging gender discrimination and violence.

Two contemporary formats of women groups hold similarities with aspects of group coaching. However, they are not solely focused on individual learning and include collective action.

Employee resource groups and women affinity groups

About one third of companies have created formal employee resource groups (ERG). The main purpose of these groups is to offer professional development opportunities targeted to a specific employee group in service of the organization's objectives. Attitudes towards gender-based ERG vary, with some companies viewing it as a safe space, others viewing it as divisive.

Women affinity groups are informal and not tied to the employer's objectives. They are much more prevalent than ERG. They exist to foster a sense of belonging and community among women. Some women affinity groups are open to men.

Both types of groups may offer multiple learning opportunities for women, such as networking events, book groups, workshops focused on a specific leadership skill, including how to respond to micro-aggressions.

Research on the effectiveness of these groups is limited. Benefits for the organization include talent acquisition, retention, and engagement. Members of ERGs report experiencing a greater sense of community, enhanced communication skills, and sense of meaningfulness.

Women's circles: a laboratory of effective membership

Women's circles emerged with the feminist spirituality movement of the 1970s. They are not hierarchical, are non-linear, and typically focused on women's agency and power through the cultivation of their strengths and resilience. These groups are typically formed outside of organizations. They provide a space for women to engage in healing and restorative activities such as meditation, storytelling, or rituals. Some circles are self-managed, and some are facilitated. Members do not know each other when they join the circle and tend not to interact with each other outside of the circle.

Women's circles have influenced the practice of group coaching. Of particular interest are methods that bond the group by creating a sense of sisterhood including connectedness and solidarity. Examples of methods that have been adapted include opening and closing techniques, holding space, absence of advice and judgement, grounding approaches, inclusive communication, non-competitiveness, and surfacing common topics for the purpose of collective reflection.

Benefits of women-only groups

The proponents of mixed-gender membership draw from theories of social learning and cognitive development to argue that women participants will benefit more from them than from women-only membership. They claim that women become more resourceful and develop themselves with agency rather than being confined within the perceived limitations of their circumstances. Another advantage is that it educates men about gender bias and other structural challenges faced by women in organizations, which promotes inclusive leadership. Arguably, men are more likely to be in position of power than women to enact changes: it's best to get them involved. In other research, some women have reported feeling that women-only learning experiences may be career damaging by giving the perception that they need extra help to succeed. Another perspective is that, since one main outcome of a group learning experience is the development of networks, it would limit opportunities for women if men were not invited.

The proponents of women-only approaches draw from empirical research in group therapy and in leadership development programs. In psychotherapy research, the evidence indicates that women speak less in mixed-gender group than in women-only groups. A possible interpretation is that women feel less psychologically safe in mixed-gender settings. This leads to weaker group cohesion which in turn might affect personal outcomes for the members. Leadership development research indicates that in mixed-gender settings gendered expectations play out and adversely impact safety for women participants. As a result, women tend to hold back when sharing their experience and are less likely to experience transformational learning. In women-only leadership development programs participants feel psychologically safe. Consequently, they are more likely to unpack challenges and recognize those that are linked to the prevalence of masculine leadership norms.

Moreover, research on the benefits of women-only leadership development programs reports that some of the learning outcomes match more closely those that are more frequently requested by women, including greater confidence, sense of agency and networking. The research also surfaces these programs put more emphasis on relational learning, which is the preferred style of most women.

In addition to a preference for a relational approach in learning, women are more likely to display leadership style preferences that ensure bonding and agreement in a group. Such style is foundational to successful outcomes in group coaching, including transformational learning.

Arguably, women are more likely to promote coordination and cohesion, relationship building, interactive and participative preferences. This creates communality and supports the bonding of the group. Additionally, aspects of transformational leadership such as the individualization of support, inspiration, nurturing, and stakeholder orientation, provide a path to creating sustainable insights for group members.

Finally, individual behaviors that contribute to strong group dynamics have been observed more frequently in women than in men in 360-evaluations. They include:

- concern for the well-being of others
- positive affirmation of others
- eclectic and situational approaches to influence
- solution-orientation
- personal integrity – alignment with core values
- empathy and compassion
- emotional regulation
- humility
- social weaving
- inclusivity
- vulnerability
- sharing experiences

Application and benefits of group coaching

Group coaching is versatile and can be used in many different settings and for different purposes. The below list has been compiled from the review of empirical research:

- school administrators in a district construct their leadership identity
- women senior leaders from different organizations break their isolation and develop life-long peer support
- women middle managers in a large organization develop self-confidence and self-efficacy
- middle managers use solution focused coaching to address their key leadership challenge
- senior leaders discover and practice their authentic leadership
- as a part of a leadership development program, middle managers practice peer coaching skills

- middle managers set goals based on the debrief their 360 assessments using a strengths-based approach
- students in higher education use appreciative inquiry to recognize and address burnout

As this list shows, group coaching can be used as a standalone intervention or as a module of a leadership development program. It can either address a specific developmental topic or a leadership development in a more holistic way. Finally, it can happen internally within a large organization (on the condition that participants do not know each other) or it can include participants from different organizations.

While the research on group coaching is still scarce, there is an increasingly stronger body of evidence to support its effectiveness, as reported in Table 1.2 below.

Table 1.2 A typology of the benefits of group coaching reported by group coaching participants (men, women, or mixed-gender) in peer-reviewed research literature.

Type of benefit	Examples reported in research
Healing, wellbeing, reconnection to humaneness, sense of community	Empathy from group members, confidentiality, vulnerability and safety, transparency, trust & support, universality, altruism, group cohesiveness, deeper sense of connection, belonging, gratitude, tolerance of differences, universality, reduction of stress, catharsis
Cognitive change (change of mental models and thinking)	Perspective taking, normalization of challenges, vicarious learning, increased emotional intelligence (including self-awareness and interpersonal sensitivity), installation of hope, self-efficacy, self-compassion, additive creativity, boosted self-confidence, emotion regulation, trust building, acceptance and integration of one's identities, authenticity, gratitude, forgiveness, humility, meaning making, surfacing and holding paradox, system thinking, improved awareness of inter-cultural and cross-cultural differences, collective leadership
Behavioral change	Self-regulation, constructive conflict resolution, creative solutions, appreciation of alignment of goals, strengths and values, greater commitment to goals, accountability, increased competence (by practicing new skills), opportunity to practice in a safe space, giving and receiving feedback, risk-taking, development of coaching skills
Other tangible benefits	Durable social capital and network, knowledge gained from mutual imparting of information

Evidence-based group coaching practices

The group coach curious about which approaches to use will be offered hundreds of tips and tools. Most of these are anecdotal, neither explicit about their underlying theory, nor backed up by scientific evidence.

In this section, I will review models that are theoretically anchored, and evidence based. That being said, there are limitations to the quality of the research that are important to mention. Indeed, most research has been qualitative and has yet to uncover in which situation these techniques are the most adequate. In some interventions the topics discussed by the women are pre-determined by the commissioner of the group coaching intervention. Additionally, some of the research is conducted in the context of mixed interventions that combine group coaching with individual coaching and or leadership-skill development training.

There are two main approaches to group coaching: the Balint group and the Action Learning group. The practitioner will typically superimpose a coaching model to their chosen approach.

Approaches

The Balint group got its name from the founder of psychoanalysts' communities of practice that started in the 50s. The prescribed process consists in five stages:

- presenter explains the issue
- clarifying questions from the group
- group discusses – presenter listens (sometimes it is asked that the presenter turn their back to the group to facilitate the process)
- presenter shares key take-aways
- group (including presenter) review the experience

In Action Learning groups, the process is the same, with the notable exception that the presenter is invited to participate in the group discussion. The Action Learning group (or T-group) was pioneered by Lewin (1951) to help members use feedback as a trigger to change and strengthen their resourcefulness.

Models

Once the group coach has chosen a preferred approach, they have a few models of group coaching to choose from, which are largely drawn from dyadic coaching models. I will give more information about how to use some of these models in Chapter 4:

- Goal, Reality, Options, Will – GROW (Whitmore, 2002)
- psychodynamic (Kets de Vries, 2006)
- solution focused (Palmer & Whybrow, 2008)
- appreciative inquiry (Cooperrider, 1986)
- narrative coaching (Drake, 2018)
- Theory U (Sharmer, 2007)
- motivational interviewing (Miller & Rollnick, 2001)
- visual exploration (Palus & Horth, 2008)

Table 1.3 below describes the evidence collected about the effectiveness of approaches and models in group coaching. It summarizes a selection of research I uncovered on organizational group coaching for the period 2008–2023.

Conditions for effective group coaching

Groups are complex adaptive systems. In other words, they are emergent and dynamic. It is therefore impossible to fully capture how they function using standard models of causality. However, the process can be conceptualized, most notably by studying common factors or conditions, which, if they are in place, are more likely to lead to desired outcomes. There is very little research that has explored common factors of success in group coaching. Figure 1.1 below proposes a chart that summarizes the conditions that need to be in place for a successful group coaching intervention. We will start the exploration of this chart from the bottom up.

Characteristics of group members

The characteristics of members, such as their emotional fluency or learning style is likely to act as a moderator of group coaching effectiveness. However, this is yet to be evidenced in research. Group dynamics theoretical research is currently developing approaches to disaggregate the effect of the individual and of the group on the individual outcomes.

Actions of the coach: group formation and group support

Group contracting has been identified in qualitative studies of group coaching as important to support safety and mutual trust in the group.

Table 1.3 A review of group coaching models. (qual = qualitative research; quant = quantitative research; qual, quant = mixed-methods research)

Participants	Design	Model	Outcome and type of research method	Source
School leaders	6 members, 1 coach, 3 × ½ day sessions	Balint group – GROW model – pre-selected topics: leadership challenge, leadership style, relationship challenge	Construction of leadership identity (qual)	Aas & Vavik (2015)
Women Leaders	6 members, 2 coaches, 6 × 4-hour sessions	Action Learning group – solution focused – coach then group – pre-selected topics based on women leadership research	Increased capacity managing relationships and balance (qual)	Bonneywell & Gannon (2022)
School leaders	5/6 members, 1 coach, 3 × 1-day sessions	Balint group – GROW model – pre-selected topics Session 1: 360 debrief, Session 2: personal agency, Session 3: leadership development plan	Self-efficacy, role clarity (qual)	Brandmo et al. (2021)
School leaders	4/6 participants – 4 to 12 sessions	Balint group – Action planning	Satisfaction, goal setting, action plan (qual)	Flückiger et al. (2017)
Adults	6/7 members, 1 coach, 1 × 90-min session	Action Learning group – Narrative – pre-selected topics on creativity. Phase 1: sharing current experience. Phase 2: pair and group reflection on topic 1 – Phase 3: pair and individual reflection on topic 2 – Phase 4: group reflection	Increased clarity and self-efficacy (qual)	Fumoto (2016)

(Continued)

Table 1.3 (Continued)

Participants	Design	Model	Outcome and type of research method	Source
Senior leaders	5/6 members, 3 × ½-day sessions	Balint group. Open-ended questions – pre-selected topics: past / present / future Narrative coaching	Increased score on authenticity scale (quant)	Fusco et al. (2016)
Women leaders	5/8 participants – 6 sessions over 14 months – 4 hours	Action Learning group – themes: building trust, self-belief, self-esteem, presence, becoming a challenger, authentic leadership brand Sharing of challenges	Universality Insights for career growth and career development Trusted network (qual)	Gray et al. (2019)
Dept Heads Public sector	6 people, 4 × ½-day sessions	Action Learning group – GROW model – Session 1: leadership topic chosen by each participant – Sessions 2–4: follow-ups, challenges, and next steps	Increased self-awareness, courage (qual)	Gyllensten et al. (2020)
Women human service professionals	6/7 participants, 6 × 2-hour sessions	Action learning – sharing of challenges	Confidence, work engagement, self-awareness, interpersonal skills, mutual accountability (qual)	Hopkins et al. (2022)
Leaders	6 members, 4 × 90-minute sessions	Theme: Leading in a Virtual World Action learning Sharing of challenges	Increased well-being, expressing vulnerability, appreciation, acceptance, social capital, altruism (qual)	McCarthy & Ertubey (2023)

Students in a master's Program	6 participants, 4 × 90-minute sessions	Action learning Sharing of challenge	Safety, connection, self-awareness, perspective taking (qual)	Nacif (2023)
Managers	6/8 participants, 12 hours across 2 days	Action learning – positive psychology and goal setting Sharing of challenge	Reflective self-development, acceptance, proactivity, decrease in emotional costs associated with self-awareness (quant)	Sutton & Crobach (2022)
Senior leaders	5 members, 1 × 1-day session	Action Learning group using drawing and motivational interviewing	Transformational growth (qual, quant)	Ward (2008)

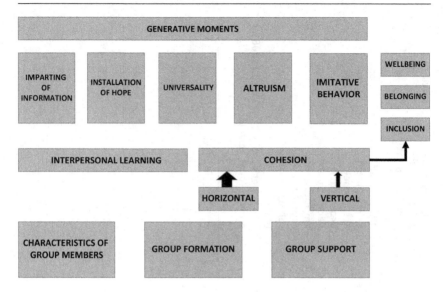

Figure 1.1 The conditions of an effective group coaching intervention.

Hackman (2012) explored the conditions that are conducive to effective group interaction (not just in group coaching, but in general). He proposed that 60% of the difference in how well a group perform is due to the preparatory work which goes into the formation of a group; 30% of the difference is the quality of the launch of the group; 10% is the action of the group leader once the group is launched. In other words, the impact of the group leader is mostly felt in the early stages of the group, whereas the group has the most impact after that.

Hodge and Clutterbuck (2019) who mapped out the common factors and conditions of effective group supervision, identified four factors that relate to the actions of the leader:

- preparatory work (examples: selection of participants, rules of engagement)
- group contracting with members (examples: practicalities, confidentiality)
- capabilities (example: co-creating safety and trust, managing self in group)
- methods, models, and frameworks

As I mentioned in the introductory chapter, little research has been done about the capacities, competencies, and skills necessary to be an effective group coach. The most important coach accrediting body, the International Coach Federation, has yet to produce an accreditation model. This is an important emerging topic for the discipline which I will discuss in the final chapter of the book.

Cohesion and interpersonal learning

Brandmo (cited in Table 1.3 above) explored the relevance of the common therapeutic factors' framework to group coaching. Using a method called content analysis, the research team analysed participants' reflection notes and written evaluations of the group coaching program, to find support for the common factors' framework. While there are limitations to the research that may not permit generalisation, seven common factors stand out in group coaching. The first two are foundational and five emerge once the first two are in place.

Interpersonal Learning

Interpersonal learning is the experience of an improved emotional landscape as a result of being part of a social microcosm. For example, participants may experience a better ability to express vulnerability, appreciation, or acceptance.

Cohesion

As I mentioned above, cohesion represents both the nature and the quality of the multiple types of relationships that develop in a group. Vertical cohesion refers to the relationships between each individual member and the leader. Horizontal cohesion represents member-to-member and member-to-group relationships.

Transformational learning theory argues that the pre-condition of cohesion, safety, is created in a holding environment bounded by norms and artifacts. Additionally, neuro-leadership research indicates that generative moments are reinforced through collaborative learning where knowledge and insights are shared and reflected upon.

The foundational importance of group cohesion has also been studied in relation to inclusion, belonging, and wellbeing.

The emerging qualitative body of research in group coaching supports the claim that horizontal cohesion is more potent than vertical cohesion in the success of a group coaching intervention. Indeed, it surfaces that the strengths of mutual participants' relationships as expressed through rapport and bonding facilitates learning and self-concept and increases social capital.

Five additional factors

Once interpersonal learning and group cohesion are present, they anchor the emergence of five additional factors: installation of hope, universality (normalization, the discovery that you are not alone and that other participants share a similar experience), imparting of information, altruism and imitate behavior.

When group coaching is not the best option

Despite its clear advantages, research has surfaced that group coaching is not always the most adequate choice for women leadership development purposes.

Group coaching is more difficult to implement than other women leadership development initiatives because it is more constrained. One of the key tenants of group coaching is that participants do not know each other so that conflicts of loyalty are avoided. Within very large international organizations these requirements may be met but this requires careful and coordinated curation. Most organizations will not have enough women leaders in their ranks who do not know each other. They will need to recommend them for an open enrollment group coaching program.

Gray et al. (2019) interviewed women leaders about their perceptions of the contrasting benefits offered by individual and group coaching. They found out that group coaching was perceived as complementary to individual coaching, not as a substitute for it. Specifically, participants report taking ideas from the group coaching back to their individual coaching sessions. This makes sense considering that less time is devoted to each participant's particular leadership challenge in group coaching. Even less time is dedicated to goal achievement. Group coaching covers an overlapping, but different spectrum of insights than dyadic coaching. In group coaching, learning occurs in a more serendipitous manner through a panel of members who have different abilities to coach. Additional learning occurs vicariously when helping other members. The implication is that organizations should not expect that group coaching will be an effective way to save costs by substituting it to one-on-one coaching.

Group coaching may perpetuate systemic discrimination. Some groups may not be able to reflect deeply about inclusivity because there is not enough diversity within them. This is in fact more likely to happen at top leadership levels where the diversity of social identities is smaller than in the general population. In addition, some group coaches may not have received enough training and supervision to fully develop their inclusive practice and may bring their own unexplored biases to their role.

Group coaching is not for everyone. When interviewing potential group members, the curator of the group should pay particular attention to the following.

- Some people learn better individually than in groups. Certain personality or cultural traits, when they are very pronounced, make it harder for a group participant to make the most of a collaborative learning experience. Overly competitive participants will derail the bonding of the group.

Participants who have a looser concept of time and commitment will not integrate well in the group. Overly extroverted participants who struggle to speak in a concise manner will not feel supported and may discourage other participants to contribute.

- The timing might not be right for some participants. Deep learning is characterized by a phase of disruption and personal discomfort before it leads to a new insight. For various reasons, an individual might not be able to handle the discomfort at this moment in their life and reject the opportunity to learn.
- Individuals who are working to overcome mental health challenges are likely to receive more help from group psychotherapy.
- People who are hoping to address a very specific and time-bounded leadership challenge (for example: conducting a job search) and are not interested in exploring anything else should be offered specialized coaching or directed to an affinity group. In a similar vein, aspiring group members who expect to receive technical or functional advice (for example, how to get funding for a start-up) should be recommended for an adequate training or a relevant community of practice.
- For women leaders, group coaching is not a substitute for networking. While group coaching has been described as one way to augment one's network, the best networking approach is not opportunistic. It starts with a leadership vision that drives an analysis and activation of the networks that fulfil it. As we will see later in the book, group coaching can be a space to learn and get new insights on how to do this.
- Finally, some women leaders need to focus on leadership development topics which require in-depth reflection and are better suited to dyadic executive coaching.

There is still very little research about group coaching benefits and how they are achieved. Group coaching is not recommended for decision makers who must justify leadership development expenses through a cost-benefit analysis. Buyers of training or executive coaching are better equipped to deliver a financial business case, because there are evidenced-based metrics who do not yet exist in group coaching.

There is no incentive for group coaching practitioners to engage in training or certification. Tellingly, the International Coaches Federation has not developed a competency model and accreditation process for group coaches. Many group coaching practitioners leverage their expertise either as a facilitator, as a dyadic or as a team coach and learn along the way as they build their practice. This leads to a lack of consistency in practice, making it even more difficult for the buyer of group coaching to find the right fit.

Reflective questions about Chapter 1

- Which type of organizational feminist theory do you find yourself closest to, and why?
- How does this influence the way you recruit group coaches or practice group coaching?
- Which of the root disciplines of group coaching are you most interested to learn more about?
- Which evidenced applications or benefits of group coaching have you witnessed? What surprised you in the list that was presented?
- Do you agree that women appear more effective than men in group coaching? If not, what evidence do you have to support your claim?
- What is your informed opinion about the respective roles of the group leader and group members in the success of an intervention?
- Have you experienced situations when group coaching was not a good choice for the development of women leaders? What happened and what have learned from this experience?
- What other reflections and questions came up after reading this chapter?

Bibliography

Aas, M., & Vavik, M. (2015). Group coaching: A new way of constructing leadership identity? *School Leadership & Management*, 35(3), 251–265.

Adams, S. J. (2023). Women have leadership advantages – on why that matters and how it may help us. *Australasian Psychiatry*, 10398562231153004.

Alldredge, C. T., Burlingame, G. M., Yang, C., & Rosendahl, J. (2021). Alliance in group therapy: A meta-analysis. *Group Dynamics: Theory, Research, and Practice*, 25(1), 13.

Berta, W., Cranley, L., Dearing, J. W., Dogherty, E. J., Squires, J. E., & Estabrooks, C. A. (2015). Why (we think) facilitation works: Insights from organizational learning theory. *Implementation Science*, 10(1), 1–13.

Bierema, L. L., Sim, E., He, W., & Cox, A. B. (2022). Double jeopardy: The paradox and promise of coaching women leaders from a critical feminist perspective. *Gender in Management: An International Journal*, 38(2), 255–271.

Bonneywell, S., & Gannon, J. (2022). Maximising female leader development through simultaneous individual and group coaching. *Coaching: An International Journal of Theory, Research and Practice*, 15(2), 180–196.

Brandmo, C., Aas, M., Colbjørnsen, T., & Olsen, R. (2021). Group coaching that promotes self-efficacy and role clarity among school leaders. *Scandinavian Journal of Educational Research*, *65*(2), 195–211.

Brown, S. W., & Grant, A. M. (2010). From GROW to GROUP: Theoretical issues and a practical model for group coaching in organisations. *Coaching: An International Journal of Theory, Research and Practice*, *3*(1), 30–45.

Buckley, H., Steinert, Y., Regehr, G., & Nimmon, L. (2019). When I say… community of practice. *Medical Education*, *53*(8), 763–765.

Burlingame, G. M., McClendon, D. T., & Yang, C. (2018). Cohesion in group therapy: A meta-analysis. *Psychotherapy*, *55*(4), 384.

Campuzano, M. V. (2019). Force and inertia: A systematic review of women's leadership in male-dominated organizational cultures in the United States. *Human Resource Development Review*, *18*(4), 437–469.

Cooperrider, D. L. (1986). *Appreciative inquiry: Toward a methodology for understanding and enhancing organizational innovation (theory, social, participation)* (Doctoral dissertation, Case Western Reserve University).

Cserti, R. (2019). Essential facilitation skills for an effective facilitator. *Delivery Matters*.

De-Valle, P. J. (2014). *An Exploration of Executive Women's Experiences of Coaching and Mentoring: An Interpretative Phenomenological Analysis Study* (Doctoral dissertation, Oxford Brookes University).

Debebe, G., Anderson, D., Bilimoria, D., & Vinnicombe, S. M. (2016). Women's leadership development programs: Lessons learned and new frontiers. *Journal of Management Education*, *40*(3), 231–252.

DeChant, B. E. (1996). *Women and group psychotherapy: Theory and practice*. Guilford Press.

De Vries, M. F. K. (2006). *The leader on the couch: A clinical approach to changing people and organizations*. John Wiley & Sons.

Drake, D. B. (2018). What story are you in? Four elements of a narrative approach to formulation in coaching. In *Constructing stories, telling tales* (pp. 239–258). Routledge.

Feghali, A. (2022). Executive peer advisory groups: Who they are? What are their benefits? Why do members join and stay? *Dissertations* 930. https://digital.sandiego.edu/cgi/viewcontent.cgi?article=1935&context=dissertations

Flückiger, B., Aas, M., Nicolaidou, M., Johnson, G., & Lovett, S. (2017). The potential of group coaching for leadership learning. *Professional Development in Education*, *43*(4), 612–629.

Fumoto, E. (2016). Developing a group coaching model to cultivate creative confidence. *International Journal of Evidence Based Coaching & Mentoring*.

Fusco, T., O'Riordan, S., & Palmer, S. (2016). Assessing the efficacy of authentic leadership group-coaching. *International Coaching Psychology Review*, *11*(2), 118–128.

Gipson, A. N., Pfaff, D. L., Mendelsohn, D. B., Catenacci, L. T., & Burke, W. W. (2017). Women and leadership: Selection, development, leadership style, and performance. *The Journal of Applied Behavioral Science*, *53*(1), 32–65.

Gray, D., De Haan, E., & Bonneywell, S. (2019). Coaching the 'ideal worker': Female leaders and the gendered self in a global corporation. *European Journal of Training and Development*, *43*(7/8), 661–681.

Grosser, K., & Moon, J. (2019). CSR and feminist organization studies: Towards an integrated theorization for the analysis of gender issues. *Journal of Business Ethics*, *155*, 321–342.

Gyllensten, K., Henschel, C., & Jones, G. (2020). The experience of executive group coaching–A qualitative study. *International Coaching Psychology Review*, *15*(1), 37–43.

Hackman, J. R. (2012). From causes to conditions in group research. *Journal of Organizational Behavior*, *33*(3), 428–444.

Hagen, M. S., Bialek, T. K., & Peterson, S. L. (2017). The nature of peer coaching: Definitions, goals, processes and outcomes. *European Journal of Training and Development*, *41*(6), 540–558.

Hideg, I., & Shen, W. (2019). Why still so few? A theoretical model of the role of benevolent sexism and career support in the continued underrepresentation of women in leadership positions. *Journal of Leadership & Organizational Studies*, *26*(3), 287–303.

Hirudayaraj, M., & Shields, L. (2019). Feminist theory: A research agenda for HRD. *Advances in Developing Human Resources*, *21*(3), 319–334.

Hodge, A., & Clutterbuck, D. (2019). Guidelines for team coach supervision. In *Coaching supervision* (pp. 161–175). Routledge.

Hopkins, K., Meyer, M., Afkinich, J., Bialobrzeski, E., Perry, V., & Brown, J. (2022). Facilitated peer coaching among women human service professionals: Leadership learning, application and lessons learned. *Human Service Organizations: Management, Leadership & Governance*, *46*(3), 184–201.

Kets de Vries, M. F. (2014). The group coaching conundrum. *International Journal of Evidence Based Coaching and Mentoring*, *12*(1), 79–91.

Knight, C. (2017). The mutual aid model of group supervision. *The Clinical Supervisor*, *36*(2), 259–281.

Lewin, K. (1951). Intention, will and need. In D. Rapaport, *Organization and pathology of thought: Selected sources* (pp. 95–153). Columbia University Press.

Lewis, P., Adamson, M., Biese, I., & Kelan, E. (2019). Introduction to special issue: Exploring the emergence of moderate feminism(s) in contemporary organizations. *Gender, Work and Organization*.

Mangione, L., & Forti, R. (2018). Beyond midlife and before retirement: A short-term women's group. *International Journal of Group Psychotherapy*, *68*(3), 314–336.

McCarthy, S., & Ertubey, C. (2023). Understanding relationships in online group coaching for leaders working remotely in Canada: An interpretative phenomenological analysis. *International Journal of Evidence Based Coaching & Mentoring*, *21*(1).

Miller, W. R., & Rollnick, S. (2001). When is it motivational interviewing? *Addiction-Abingdon*, *96*(12), 1770–1771.

Nacif, A. P., Giraldez-Hayes, A., Finn, K., & Valdivielso-Martínez, E. (2023). Online group coaching: The experience of postgraduate students during the COVID-19 pandemic. *Coaching: An International Journal of Theory, Research and Practice*, 1–15.

Ostrowski, E. (2019). Using group coaching to foster reflection and learning in an MBA classroom. *Philosophy of Coaching: An International Journal*, *4*(2), 53–74.

Ozkazanc-Pan, B. (2019). On agency and empowerment in a #MeToo world. *Gender, Work & Organization, 26*(8), 1212–1220.

Palmer, S. E., & Whybrow, A. E. (2008). *Handbook of coaching psychology: A guide for practitioners.* Routledge.

Palus, C., & Horth, D. (2008). About visual explorer. *The change handbook (Volume 3 of 4) (EasyRead Super Large 18pt Edition)*, 394. Center of Creative Leadership.

Paré, D. (2016). Creating a space for acknowledgment and generativity in reflective group supervision. *Family Process, 55*(2), 270–286.

Perriton, L. (2022). The problematic persistence of gender reflexivity in women's leadership development. *Journal of Management Development, 41*(5), 335–347.

Pierli, G., Murmura, F., & Palazzi, F. (2022). Women and leadership: How do women leaders contribute to companies' sustainable choices? *Frontiers in Sustainability, 3*, 930116.

Sharmer, C. O. (2007). Theory U. *Learning from the future as it emerges.* Berrett-Koehler Publishers.

Steinberg, B., & Watkins, M. D. (2021). The surprising power of peer coaching. *Harvard Business Review.*

Sutton, A., & Crobach, C. (2022). Improving self-awareness and engagement through group coaching. *International Journal of Evidence Based Coaching & Mentoring, 20*(1). 10.24384/dqtf-9x16

Talik, W., Wiechetek, M., & Dean, A. Competency profile of coach – ComTal-Group Coach.

Tasca, G. A. (2021). Twenty-five years of group dynamics: Theory, research and practice: Introduction to the special issue. *Group Dynamics: Theory, Research, and Practice, 25*(3), 205.

Thomas, G., & Thorpe, S. (2019). Enhancing the facilitation of online groups in higher education: a review of the literature on face-to-face and online group-facilitation. *Interactive Learning Environments, 27*(1), 62–71.

Thornton, C. (2010). *Group and team coaching: The essential guide.* Routledge.

Whitmore, J. (2002). *Coaching for performance* (Vol. 108). London: Nicholas Brealey Publishing.

Van der Veen, N., & Reid, A. (2021). *Amplifying personal and leadership development through group coaching.* Gordon Institute of Business Science, University of Pretoria.

Van Dyke, P. R. (2014). Virtual group coaching: A curriculum for coaches and educators. *Journal of Psychological Issues in Organizational Culture, 5*(2), 72–86.

Ward, G. (2008). Towards executive change: A psychodynamic group coaching model for short executive programmes. *International Journal of Evidence Based Coaching & Mentoring, 6*(1), 67–68.

Wenger, E. (1998). Communities of practice: Learning as a social system. *Systems Thinker, 9*(5), 2–3.

Yalom, I. D., & Leszcz, M. (2020). *The theory and practice of group psychotherapy.* Basic Books.

Chapter 2

The Experience of Women Leaders in Group Coaching

Key points of Chapter 2

✓ The main stakeholders of group coaching are the group, the members, and the group coach. They each come to an intervention influenced by the systems they operate in.

✓ A coaching group experiences stages of forming, storming, norming, performing, and adjourning which have been identified in group theory and research.

✓ When women leaders join a group, the benefits they seek are very aligned with those that have been surfaced in research.

✓ After the first session, the benefits of group coaching are mostly related to wellbeing. After three sessions, wellbeing is still predominant, though benefits related to cognitive change, such as new insights, personal growth, or normalization start to emerge. It takes about nine sessions for the benefits related to cognitive change to take precedence over the wellbeing benefits.

✓ Most topics brought to group coaching relate to managing oneself (wellbeing, career management, owning my power, purpose). Managing relationships is in second place (team management, managing up, difficult people, visibility, influence, and feedback). Topic related to managing the organization come third (organizational development, change management, DEI).

✓ In a high-functioning group, the main event triggering the ending of a group membership is the cessation of sponsorship by the commissioner.

DOI: 10.4324/9781003465195-3

Purpose of Chapter 2

In his poem *The Student's Prayer*, Humberto Maturana exhorts his teacher to listen to him rather than to themselves, so that he can be himself as a learner rather than what the teacher wants him to be. As a client-centered coach, I profoundly believe that the group coach is not an expert, nor a teacher, but a partner to the group. I work with the group members to define what process is most likely to match the group's needs, adjusting along the way.

This chapter is centered on an exploration of the experience of the women leaders, from the moment they make the decision to enrol in group coaching until they decide to end the journey. This exploration is based on a thematic analysis of the self-reflective notes that I have used over the last 15 years for the purpose of my professional development. The thematic analysis uses a critical realist framework. This means that I have analysed all my notes to identify themes that reflect the antecedents, the process, and the outcome of group coaching. In this chapter, I focus on the notes that I have captured to better understand the perspective of the group members.

The thematic analysis is based on my note taking of the reported experiences of approximately 200 women leaders worldwide who have been members of groups that I have coached since 2009. Approximately 50% of these members are based in North America, 25% in Europe and 25% in Southeast Asia. Over 50 nationalities are represented. All the case studies presented in this chapter and the following ones are composite, which preserves the privacy of group members as well as the confidential nature of the group's conversations.

To set the stage, I begin with a presentation of the stakeholders of group coaching and of the systems that they operate in. Subsequently, I consider the life cycle of the group to introduce an exploration of the members' experience. The thematic analysis explores the hopes and expectations of the members, the perceived benefits of group coaching over time, the most frequent topics that women leaders bring to group coaching, and their key reasons to leave a group.

Stakeholders of group coaching and their system

A group coaching intervention involves at least three stakeholders: a group coach, individual members, and a group. As shown in Figure 2.1, each stakeholder of the group coaching intervention operates within a system that influences how they are going to feel, act and interact during the intervention. The group coach is represented by the women conductor, the participants by the other women, and the star evokes the group. In this section we will review each stakeholder's system.

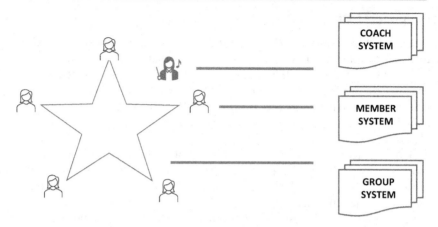

Figure 2.1 The stakeholders of a group intervention and their respective systems.

The system of the group coach

The system of the group coach may include the commissioner, typically the Human Resources leader who represents the organization that sponsors a group member. It may also include a coaching service provider who is contracted by the organization to deliver the group coaching intervention.

The group coach may either be a contractor or an employee of the organization that commissions the group coaching. The same applies to the relationship between the coaching service provider and the group coach.

In dyadic coaching, the distinction is made between internal coaching and external coaching, and the position of the coach is central to it. A coach employed in the same organization as their client is internal. Otherwise, they are an external coach. In group coaching one needs to consider two levels: whether the group members are all employed by the same the organization, and whether the group coach is employed by the same organization as them.

The scholarly literature on group coaching has nothing to say about the pros and cons of internal vs. external group coaching. Schalk and Landeta (2017) based on a literature review and a survey of experts reviewed the pros and cons of internal vs. external dyadic executive coaching. If we infer their findings about dyadic executive coaching to group coaching, here are some possible considerations.

Internal group coaching is likely to include reflections about the organization's needs and how they interface with the group members' learning objectives. For example, internal coaching groups might be viewed as an opportunity to transmit the company's culture, especially if some group members are newcomers. Internal coaching groups might be used to deepen the group members' understanding about the company culture and how it impacts the common challenges that they are facing. Some groups may evolve to explore a collective engagement to change organizational practices, in which case they might shift to a team coaching process. Internal group coaching is more likely to generate conflicts of loyalty or conflicts of interest within the group. We will see later in the book that it adds a challenge to the cohesion of the group. In contrast, external group coaching is grounded in the individual members' learning objectives. It provides a greater sense of confidentiality, psychological safety, and trust building. Table 2.1 below compares the characteristics of internal and external group coaching.

Table 2.1 Characteristics of internal and external group coaching

Internal Group Coaching	External Group Coaching	
The group coach is employed by the commissioner	The group coach is an independent contractor	
The group members are employed by the commissioner	The group members come from different organizations	
The group coach needs to manage potential conflicts of loyalty or interest between members, as well as between herself and the members	The group coach has latitude to eliminate conflict of loyalty and interest between the group members, and between herself and the group member	
	Coaching service provider	*Independent group coach*
The commissioner decides the purpose of the group	The coaching service provider defines the purpose of the group	The group coach defines the purpose of the group
The commissioner decides who is a member. Members may or may not participate voluntarily	Each individual member decides if want to participate	Each individual member decides if they want to participate
The commissioner curates the group and sets the parameters of the intervention	The coaching service provider curates the group and sets the parameters of the intervention	The group coach curates the groups and sets the parameters of the intervention
The commissioner sponsors the group coaching intervention	Members may either pay out-of-pocket or be sponsored by their employer	Members may either pay out-of-pocket or be sponsored by their employer
The commissioner may monitor the quality of the intervention	The coaching provider may monitor the quality of the intervention	The group coach may monitor the quality of the intervention

The internal group coach's most complex challenge is to manage psychological safety. Indeed, the likelihood of conflicts of loyalties in any given group is higher. It might impact impacts the cohesion of the group and, indirectly, the generation of insights for its individual members.

The external group coach's most complex challenge is to attend to alignment of purpose, delivery and expected results with other stakeholders. The first level of alignment is between themselves and the coaching service provider and/or the commissioner. The second level of alignment, also called vertical cohesion, is between themselves and the group and the group of members.

The group members' system

In addition to having unique personal and social identities, each group member will live in a different system. The system includes an immediate environment and wider environment. For example, the immediate environment of a particular member might be that of a single parent of young children, who works as a Chief Marketing Officer, and serves as the Board Chair of a not-for-profit. The wider environment of this same member might be that she is the only woman in the C-Suite and the first in their family to graduate from college.

When members are sponsored by their organization, they bring with them the system in which their employer operates. For example, the employer might decide to end their sponsorship to reduce costs.

The group's system

The coaching group might operate independently or integrated in a wider leadership development program. In the first case, the group coach needs to form the group. In an embedded intervention, the group might have been formed during a previous module of the leadership development program.

Groups might meet online, face to face, or in a hybrid format. This impacts the tools and techniques that are available to the group coach.

Group members may or may not share the same native language. There are groups where no-one speaks their native language. This impacts how concepts are shared and understood.

Group members might also sit on different time zones, which may lead to unequal levels of convenience or energy for the group members.

The life cycle of the group

There is no research about the optimal number of sessions in a group coaching intervention or about the duration and frequency of each group coaching session. In practice and in research, these parameters vary widely.

From the pragmatic stance that I have adopted in my practice, I believe that if the number of sessions, their frequency and their duration are set by the commissioner or the coaching service provider, the group coach must align with them about the design to ensure that group members experience the expected benefits of the intervention.

From that same stance, if nothing is set in advance, my recommendation is to hold monthly sessions renewable yearly, with a duration of 90 minutes to two hours depending on the number of members. Then it's up to the group to decide if this works for them after experimenting with the proposed format.

In contrast, independently of the duration of the intervention, a vast theoretical body of research exist about the life cycle of a group. If designed adequately, a group coaching intervention will go through similar stages whether it lasts one day or several years. Arguably, it is one of the most important roles of the coach, as we will see in subsequent chapters, to manage the transitions of the group from one stage to another.

Group development theories have been successfully tested in empirical research, most notably in group psychotherapy and group facilitation. In group coaching, Florent-Treacy (2009) explored the experience of the participants to the Consulting and Coaching program for Change (CCC) who spend several months in group coaching. She surfaced that the groups went through stages that have been theorized in group psychotherapy, including initial engagement and affiliation; focus on individual differentiation and competition; intimacy, engagement, and cohesion; ending of the group experience. This description echoes a four-stage model proposed by Tuckman (1965): forming, storming, norming, and performing, to which was added a fifth stage of adjourning in a later paper (1977).

These stages need to be reactivated when ruptures of group dynamic happen. These ruptures are either caused by changes experienced by individual participants (examples: change of career or personal situation), by changes in the group composition (examples: arrival or departure of participants), or by external circumstances impacting the group (example: meeting online instead of in person).

Regardless of their duration, groups will go through stages. At each group stage, the group coach invites the members to move along the journey by offering different set of activities. Table 2.2 below shows my preferred approach at the beginning, middle and end of group meeting, depending on what group stage they are in.

Table 2.2 Main activities proposed by the group coach the intersection of the group and meeting stage

Group stage →	Forming	Storming	Adjourning
Meeting stage ↓	Norming	Performing	
Beginning	Deep mutual introductions Sharing of hopes and expectations	Focused spotlight on personal characteristics Follow-ups Encouraging mutual aid	Celebration of the journey
Middle	Charter Common topics Practice group coaching	Group coaching Meta learning and process improvement	Key takeaways from the group coaching journey
End	Sharing experience	Sharing key takeaways	New beginnings

Hopes and expectations from group coaching

When women leaders enter the group coaching space, they have hopes and expectations about the journey and its benefits. They also come with some trepidation. At the end of the first session, when I ask new group members how they entered the space, some report that they felt "guilty about giving time to themselves," "nervous about the process," "anxious, unsure how this is going to work," "concerned about urgent things needing taking care of," "torn about whether or not this is the right way to use my time," "guilty about needing help," "self-conscious and afraid to share." These initial feelings typically dissipate after three sessions as the cohesion of the group develops.

In this section I will explore what these hopes and expectations are. But first, it is useful to picture a composite profile of a typical woman leader who joins the group.

A composite profile of the typical women leader who joins a coaching group

Let's call our typical participant Maria. She is 40 to 60 years old and manages either a function, a region, or a business line in a large organization. Alternatively, she leads a smaller organization. To get to this career stage, she has, from a young age, "overcome obstacles, beating the odds, doing what nobody thought she could do." She may have been a former competitive athlete. She views hardships as opportunities to learn how to "own my competence and power, strengthening my self-confidence in organizations that are still defined by male norms." Maria is driven, has ambitious career goals and defies ageist stereotypes. She like jobs that "stretch you and make you learn." Maria is a risk taker; she "raises her hand for a new challenge." She always strives to be in control, "taking charge of my destiny, being self-reliant." This has served her most of the time, however she recognizes that she "lacks peer support, relying only on myself."

When she does not have children of her own, Maria is likely to raise or financially support younger members of her extended family. Additionally, she is often the main or the sole breadwinner. If her parents are in the latest stage of their life, she is likely to take the lead managing their support system. If her parents are younger, they are an integral part of the strong support system that she has built for her loved ones.

If she is not leading a not-for-profit, Maria is likely to support a charitable cause, either as an investor or as Board member. Maria constantly operates at the limit of her current capacity. She is aware of the importance of managing her energy carefully, but she needs frequent readjustments, and sometimes feels "out of balance."

What attracts women leaders to group coaching?

The histogram in Figure 2.2 below represents the frequency of reasons cited by women leaders to join a coaching group. It is based on the members' response to the question: What are your top two hopes for group coaching?

I will discuss the findings using the same typology of benefits measured in research as presented in Table 1.2 of the previous chapter. Indeed, the themes

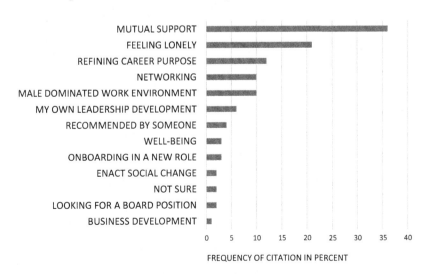

Figure 2.2 Benefits of group coaching expected by women leaders.

surfaced align well with the four types of benefits described in research: healing, wellbeing and connection, cognitive change, behavioral change, and other tangible benefits.

Healing, wellbeing, reconnection to humanness, sense of community

In this category I have included the following: feeling lonely and wellbeing. Taken together these two themes represent 22% of the responses.

Many women leaders joining a coaching group report having difficulty making time for personal relationships with others, especially with other women. They recognize lacking consistency, letting important friendships go stale because they prioritize their work and family. Fighting loneliness is an important motivator to join a coaching group because they "don't have many people to confide in," want "a community for myself," "to meet other women, make friends, get a female perspective." They realize that "I am not as connected to other women as I would like to be," "the other professional women I know are so busy."

An additional 3% view group coaching as a well-being process, as "a chance to step back," to "break the daily routine."

Cognitive change

In this category I have included mutual support, career purpose and how to thrive in working environments where men leaders are the norm.

Mutual support represents almost one third of the responses. Women leaders are looking for: "camaraderie with professionals who have the same interests," "hanging out with authentic and fearless women," "lean on each other to cultivate and nurture our confidence," "support and supporting others," "mutual giving and receiving," "the diversity of experiences and perspectives."

The opportunity to reflect on their career purpose is cited 11% of the time. Women leaders mention that "I am looking for a peer group to bounce off ideas about next career steps," noting that "my own career management has always been last."

An additional 9% of the responses express the need to navigate working environments where men leaders are the norm. Women leaders mention that "I interact mostly with men," "I report to an all-man board." They are interested in reflecting on "managing the men around us who are too competitive" or want to "surmount the likeability challenge."

Behavioral change

This need is not prevalent amongst the women leaders that I have worked with. Leadership development is cited only 5% of the time, by women leaders who are interested in "getting some best practices," "goals for myself," "mutual accountability," or "behavioral effectiveness in the corporate world."

Other tangible benefits

Networking and business development are cited 10% of the time, by women leaders who consider the group as "an opportunity to expand my female networking," "use a broader network," or "network with more senior women to help me grow my practice."

The first two needs of connection and cognitive change represent almost 80% of those cited. These findings evoke those surfaced by Gray et al. (2019) and shared in the previous chapter: women leaders use other types of leadership development intervention to implement their leadership development goals.

Another common pattern is the absence of interest in using group coaching as a platform for social change, which is cited only 2% of the time. In fact, many of the women leaders I work with are deeply committed to social change. A significant number of participants lead not-for-profits, many sit on not-for-profit boards, or volunteer in charitable organizations. Instead of using the group as a platform to bring change, they use the group to reflect on the individual leadership challenges and opportunities that stem from these activities.

Benefits experienced by women leaders

In this section, I describe the key benefits experienced by women leaders who participate in multiple group coaching sessions, and how these benefits evolve over time.

Figure 2.3 below describe the prevalence of benefits experienced by the group members who meet monthly at the end of sessions 1, 3, 6, 9, 12, 24, and 36. This is based on the answer to the question: "Which top two benefits did you experience at the end of this session?".

Connection

Connection builds very quickly and deepens over time. It continues to be cited as a key benefit even long into the group life. At the end of the first session, some members are mesmerized by the "personal connections that happened with a group of perfect strangers." They note the "easiness with which we bonded." They mention "feeling understood in the challenges I am facing with my role." They feel "admiration for the other women in the group," "moved and connected with the group." One participant wondered about the potential to foster more collaborative practices in her organization

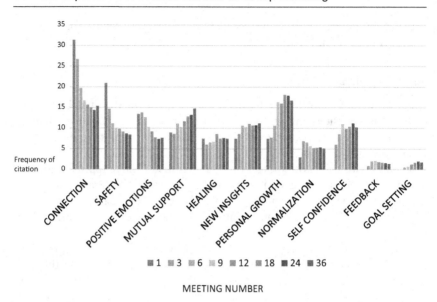

Frequency of citation

1 3 6 9 12 18 24 36

MEETING NUMBER

Figure 2.3 Benefits experienced by women leaders after a group coaching session, over time.

"Women are collaborative. We are building on this strength here and now. This makes me wonder how collaboration can get better recognized and leveraged in my organization?". Group members who have been meeting regularly for a year note describe "how quickly we became sincere, honest, humble and transparent with each other."

Connections deepen over time through shared experiences. "We have become increasingly open to sharing," "We started meeting at the start of Covid and got thrown together into it."

Safety

Safety emerges as a key benefit during the first session. Members comment that this first meeting "gave them a space to feel vulnerable" because "it's open right off the bat." "I feel at ease even though I am normally reserved and shy." The affirmation of confidentiality plays an important role in creating the safe space. At the end of her first session, a member envision the group as "a brain trust that is confidential and where I can be vulnerable." Safety continues to be appreciated over time: "I was moved by your candor. I am coming out of my hole." Many women leaders have few spaces of safety outside of the group. "This is such an incredible privilege to reflect in a safe space" and to "have the sort of conversation we cannot have with our teams." They appreciate "the absence of competition," experience "permission to cry and laugh."

Positive emotions

The sense of cohesion and the safety of the group generate many positive emotions. The experience shifts their perspective and energizes them for the rest of the day. "I feel contented by the positive spin I receive," "I feel lighter and happier," "I feel encouraged to move," I had "a chance to celebrate small wins." After a meeting, "I always feel inspired and in awe of this group."

Mutual support

As early as the first meeting, members acknowledge "the potential for mutual learning." They "sense a commitment to each other," "that everyone will benefit from it." The level of mutual support keeps growing over time.

On the receiving side, they surface that "for the first time I feel helped by a women leader," they "appreciate the framing, the listening and the sounding board" provided by other members. They notice that "the trust in our relationship allows us to dig below the surface" and share their "surprise of the power of supportive relationships."

On the giving side, women leaders mention "it's nice to know that I contributed to unlock someone," "the group is of huge help to me including when I help someone with their issue," "this is an opportunity to give and to receive," "a chance to provide insights to someone who needs them."

Healing

While not as prevalent as other benefits, healing is cited consistently regardless of the duration of the group. Members note that "I was able to take things off my chest," I feel "calmer, more comfortable." The space "gives me a break from the image that I am expected to portray." The healing benefits may be crucial to their commitment to the group, because "it is not often that I have a chance to take a pause," "it is like self-care," "at the end of each meeting I have positive energy," "the group is filling my tank," it is "a lifeline, a good shot in the arm." The group "gives me permission to recognize that emotions can be overwhelming in a crisis." It helps me see "a path to see the human side of the people I am in conflict with at work." It "helps me shed bad energy." I feel "refocused on what I can truly control: myself," and "redirected to more joyful things."

New insights

New insights start to emerge very early in the group formation through story telling. Members remark that "listening to a variety of experiences inspires me," "it helps me put things in perspective," "allow me to dissect a topic and expand my thinking." Story telling remains a potent source of inspiration throughout the group coaching experience.

New insights are strengthened by open-ended questions asked by other members when a presenter introduces a challenge. These questions act as a "springboard for me to reflect further," "help me break down and deconstruct my issue," "help clarify why things do not work out." They recognize the power of receiving questions from a group: "it brings our thinking to the next level."

Many members verbalize that they get new insights from "listening to other's challenges," that "the deep dive in someone else's challenge creates vicarious learning." They "take notes that inspire me to try new things at work."

Personal growth

Personal growth is defined as the verbalization that the member has experienced cognitive change as a result of processing new insights. It starts early on, and progressively increases over time, though it seems to peak after the 18th session.

Members describe being "a step further to where I was," notice that "the insight and advice I offer apply to myself as well." They note having become "more self-aware," "better able to use my strengths to solve an issue." "The process was progressive, the group helped me find my way forward."

At the one-year anniversary of the group, members share how Anemone has used the support of the group

Group members comments on Anemone's journey over the last year. She left a position that was not a good fit, identified a better place to thrive, and got the role she wanted:

- "She used the group's input to work on herself and to understand what she needed going forward. She pro-actively decided to make a request to her former boss to test things out. When her request was denied, she made the change happen. It's an inspiration"
- "She took the risk to transition and do it all over again. I think I would never be able to do this, but now I wonder"
- "She was the first member of the group to make herself vulnerable and make sense of the source of her frustrations in her role"

Members reflect on their own journey at the one-year mark

- "I got to know myself better. When I finally stopped to be perfectionist about the household during Covid, I realized how resilient my family was"
- "I really experimented taking risks. For the first time in my life, I tried being an investor. It worked and now I feel confident about skills"
- "I understood that it's OK to be vulnerable in this group. I am allowing myself to consider being vulnerable in other spaces"
- "I realized I don't have to be the task-master for everyone"
- "I enjoyed the process of listening and sharing my perspective in the group coaching sessions. It made me want to learn more and research about leadership topics"
- "Feeling vulnerable does not mean that you can't do something. I was willing to be transparent about my challenges and this helped me move forward"
- "I was able to protect my time for this group. This made me say no to other things. I make a conscious effort to say no when I need to replenish my energy"
- "My main success this year was to realize that I needed to step back, reflect with the group, then reflect with myself, before taking a step forward"

Normalization

As women leaders share more and more stories, there is a realization that many challenges are common. This fulfils one of the greatest hopes and expectations about the group experience: the experience of not feeling alone. Women leaders report "I thought it was only me." They appreciate "feeling energized by the commonalities," share that "I can relate to almost every story shared." "My own challenge is normalized, and I see it now in a more positive light."

Self-confidence

Self-confidence emerges as a benefit from the third session onwards. From then on, it remains an important outcome of group coaching. After receiving group coaching, members report "Feeling heard by a group of accomplished women builds my self-confidence," "I feel more capable than I had thought," "I feel encouraged," "it inspires me to be more ambitious and to take more risks." Additionally, "it helps me take control over the narrative."

Hearing stories has a beneficial impact as well. "I benefited from hearing examples of advocating for myself. I have been too much behind the scenes."

In addition, telling stories strengthens self-confidence: "story telling brings back strengths that I was no longer aware of." "I get courage and confidence based on what I have done before."

Feedback

Women leaders report that they receive little actionable feedback in their role as leaders. They are actively looking for other sources of feedback. The group offers a lot of positive reinforcement which they appreciate: "positive feedback keeps me motivated." Occasionally, members report the benefit of constructive feedback from the group: "the group called me out and woke me up," "feedback was a gift because it was given with positive intent."

Goal setting

From time to time, members report having benefited from sharing their action plan with the group, noticing that "I am inspired to commit to what I have shared with the group." Some members hold each other accountable in between sessions. I encourage each member to surface an actionable take-away at the end of each meeting and they appreciate this.

Topics surfaced by women leaders during group coaching

Figure 2.4 below describes the main topics brought by women leaders to group coaching. Most topics relate to managing self (wellbeing, career management, owning my power, purpose). Managing relationships is in second place (team management, managing up, difficult people, visibility, influence, and feedback). Topic related to managing the organization come third (organizational development, change management, Diversity, Equity, and Inclusion).

Wellbeing

Women leaders frequently use the group as a sounding board to reflect on ways they can become more accountable to themselves to manage their energy and wellbeing. Issues include: "identifying habits that get in the way

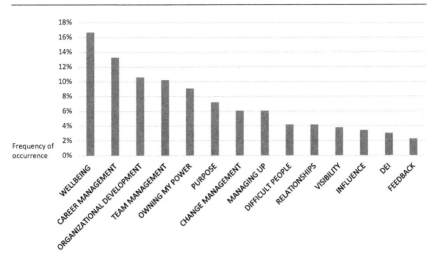

Figure 2.4 Main leadership development topics brought to group coaching by women leaders.

of achieving my wellbeing vision," "achieving more balance, time management, and better focus on self-care," "giving myself permission to enable my self-care objectives," "finding more joy and fun in what I do," "getting a grip on managing my share of mind so that there is more time for me," "getting in better shape," "making the most of my flow of business insights and ideas, while optimizing my schedule and energy," "taking care of myself when I feel drained," "proactive and reactive solutions to respond to constant solicitations," "showing vulnerability and asking for help."

Amara is an experienced partner in a professional service company. She would like to move to the managing partner role in her office. This requires maintaining a steady growth rate for the portfolio she manages, in addition to visibility-building activities inside and outside the partnership. Amara is unsure whether she will have enough energy to fight for this in the long run.

Amara's question to the group

How can I better manage my energy in my current role to give it a try?

Group's interventions

- What tools and techniques are you using to manage your energy tactically during the day?
- What would be the benefits to hire a Chief of Staff?
- What advice are you not listening to, and why?
- What tasks can you delegate and outsource?
- How clear is your vision for the managing partner role?
- Who do you need to communicate it to?
- How is your networking plan connected to your vision?

Amara's key takeaways

- I need a vision to manage my energy better
- I will be intentional about I what need to excel at, and what I don't
- I will build a strategic networking plan based on my vision

Career management

The group is perceived as an ideal space to process career management decisions. Topics brought to coaching include "building confidence in my ability to own a new, much broader role offered to me," "reflecting on the alignment between my current role and my career purpose," "balancing my time and energy between different roles," "managing my loyalty to my team and organization when it's time to leave," "managing my fear of choosing the wrong job."

Boronia has been working in the same international company for 20 years. At her level, there are few opportunities for promotion, yet she feels capable to take on more responsibilities. She has an excellent reputation in the company due to her outstanding executions skills. But she would like her next role to be more strategic.

Boronia's question to the group

How can I position myself for a more strategic role?

Group's interventions

- Internally, who knows that you want to operate more at the strategic level? Who is a trusted partner you could talk to?
- As you scan internal lateral opportunities in your current company, what projects stand out that would give you strategic visibility?
- What requirements do you have for your next role? For instance, would you be open to work as an individual contributor, or do you enjoy the role of managing large teams as you do in your current role?
- What would you lose if you articulated your career needs clearly to your boss and HR partner?
- What holds you back looking for a strategic role outside of your current company?

Boronia's key takeaways

- As a first step, I want to experiment asking to work on an internal project that requires more strategic thinking than implementation skills. I will make this request to the CEO
- To achieve this I need to scan existing projects and come up with additional suggestions to present to my boss and HR

Organizational development

After the Covid pandemic, designing and implementing a hybrid workplace has taken an oversized share of thought for women leaders. Topics include "balance employee's wellbeing and business success," "building cohesion in remote teams," "designing and implementing a hybrid working culture," "onboarding in hybrid," "rethink the office environment," "support younger employees," etc.

Genista has been the CFO of a large hospital for five months. Her role is likely to be conducted from home for the foreseeable future. She has not yet met anyone in person, including her staff. At a time when the hospital is facing multiple challenges and the administrative staff does not get a lot of recognition, her mandate is to promote engagement and increase motivation.

Genista's question to the group

How can I promote engagement and motivate my staff under such circumstances?

Group's interventions

- What steps have you taken so far to bring the staff together? What has worked well?
- What is already happening on your team that fosters engagement and motivation?
- What is your vision of high engagement within your team? Are you aligned with them?
- How aligned are you with your boss?
- How patient are you willing to be with yourself and others?
- How can you work around your at-home work status? What type of face-to-face events might be appropriate to organize face to face outside of the office?
- Do you have a business case to request a Chief of Staff? What would you like this role to do for you?
- Who can give you support within your team? How could you delegate the execution of your vision to your direct reports?
- How well do your staff know you? What story would you like to tell them that connects with your vision of engagement?

Genista's key takeaways

- I feel empowered to be more assertive to my boss and my direct report about my vision and seek alignment with them
- In the short term, I want to organize a team-meeting event outside of the office

Team management

Team management challenges revolve around "increasing psychological safety," "dealing with attrition and its impact on the team's cohesiveness and morale," "how to communicate difficult news in uncertain economic times," "conduct a restructuring in a humane way, while keeping the remaining employees motivated," "leading a team where people have widely different political views," "managing self when leading younger generations."

Cordyline is the CFO of a large professional services firm. Her team consists largely of younger Millennials and Gen Ys. More recently, she has hired Gen Z employees. While they enjoy their role and impact, they seem to be mostly motivated by rapid promotions, salaries, benefits, better work-life balance, and the quality of interpersonal relationships with other team members. She wonders if some of them are as committed to the long-term success of the business as she was at their age. Cordyline notices that she feels increasingly frustrated with them and judgmental about their life priorities. She knows this is not the right way to be.

Cordyline's question to the group

How can I shift to a more positive mood and manage my staff accordingly?

Group's interventions

- The group members notice they are also adjusting to a generation that has different life priorities than they did at their age
- Some group members report that these generations are not shy about taking the role of spokesperson or influencers when they feel that their values are violated
- Do you know who these spokespersons or influencers are on your team? How could you create a productive working relationship with them?
- How could you challenge them to collectively find and own a solution when they raise an issue?
- How could you challenge them to analyze the consequences of the behaviors you are worried about?
- Who else is experiencing similar issues on the executive team? Who could you partner with for mutual support? What is the CEO's take on this?
- Group members shared their best practices to motivate these younger generations:

  - Ask them what excites them and to take ownership of projects accordingly
  - Give them more accountability and responsibility

- Help them connect their career purpose with the business purpose
- Remind them of the company's mission
- Offer to the younger employees the options to shadow you for a day or two
- Regularly engage in managerial coaching (whether one-on-one or in small groups)

Cordyline's key takeaway

- I feel engaged and ready to write an action plan
- I am committed to be more transparent with my peers and CFO about this issue

Owning my power

Women leaders in my groups are subject to the "double bind" effect that is described in the review of the feminist organizational literature in the previous chapter. Here is how they experience it:

- "There is a perception that women are difficult to work with when they try to own their power. This makes us feel guilty. Taking a coaching approach helps, that is if the peer is coachable"
- "From the culture I come from, it's hard not to been seen as aggressive when you own your power as a female leader"
- "I am confident, driven, and direct. It's not a popularity contest and I want to stay authentic to myself. I realize that sometimes I have to be more eclectic in my behaviors and find the right balance"
- "Beating up sexism means knowing how to be heard and be given a seat at the table. In my role, I prepare decisions that are made by men. I feel invisible"
- "I could not always put my finger on the misogyny of the corporate world. The group helped me understand, in retrospect, what was going on"
- "Many women fear rejection and deceit. But we are reticent to speak up about it"

In group coaching, they bring the need to raise their share of voice, and ask other members for support: "how to manage myself and affirm my expertise when it's being invalidated by the other members of the leadership teams who are all male," "as a co-owner with a male partner, I generate 60% of the business, how can I affirm my voice on strategic matters and push back on getting overly involved with tactical matters?".

Many group members use the group as a sounding board to build self-confidence. Questions brought to the group include: "How to get rid of my fear of blind spots as I onboard in my new role?", "How to manage my imposter syndrome as I apply for corporate Board positions?", "Should I apply for a job that is a good fit with my leadership strengths but somewhat departs from my functional expertise?", "I am being considered as the GM of large business unit, how do I authentically showcase that I am the right person for the role?"

Spirea is the CMO of a mid-cap. She would like to increase her share of voice in the executive committee. Her peers tend to insert themselves into her recommendations. They complain about a lack of focus in the marketing strategy and question her credibility because she is new to the company's industry. Spirea does not think that she has the ear of the CEO. She would like to make him aware of the fact that the lack of strategic direction of the company undermines her ability to clarify the marketing strategy.

Spirea's question to the group

How can I make my voice heard?

Group's interventions

- How can you articulate your vision in a way that connects to the needs of the executive team members?
- How equipped are you to challenge the executive team to come up with a clearer strategy?
- How clear is your business case to connect your marketing budget requests with the company's success?
- What is your path to gain to reset your relationship with the CEO?
- Who are likely to be your allies? How can you enroll them into your cause?
- How strong are your working relationships with your peers? How can you strengthen them?
- What requests do you need to make in order to belong to the team?

Spirea's key takeaways

- I am committed to become the marketing confidante of my CEO
- I need to manage my time and energy differently so that I have more time to think strategically
- I have built a strong team: I can trust them to take on more

Purpose

Some members leverage the group reflect on their leadership purpose when they face important career transitions such as leaving a job or considering a job offer.

Amaryllis left a corporate finance role in a large international company a few months ago. She feels that she has one more job in her before retiring. Lately she has felt restless and impatient to find another job that continues to engage her strengths but is less demanding on her time. Due to her reputation on the market, she is receiving a steady stream of calls from head-hunters about "fixer positions," something that she does not want to do anymore. Additionally, having always used her power and influence in her former organization to help others, she finds it particularly difficult to ask for help and to network with former colleagues. She has always been the "best in class" and now she feels that she is letting herself down.

Amaryllis' question to the group

How can I turn around my job search and regain my self-confidence?

Group's interventions

- You mentioned that your professional vision was "making execution work." How does this translate in a clear career goal that matches your aspirations?
- Previously you had shared with us your passion for mentoring younger professionals. How does this connect to your career goal?

- What strengths could you bring to an advisory board, or as a consultant?
- What would it take for you to slow down, to be strategic about whom you want to ask for help and prepare for these conversations with them?

Amaryllis' key takeaways

- I realize I am too frantic
- I am committed to spend more time building my job search strategy instead of restlessly responding to head-hunter's calls
- I will investigate what a portfolio career might look like

Change management

Women leaders support themselves to reflect on "leading a culture change," "engaging the Board in an organizational development initiative," "managing resistance to a culture change."

Begonia is the executive director of a not-for-profit. In the past she has required very little support from the Board, and they are used to seeing her as the person in control. However, due to external events, it is now very clear that the organization needs to scale to stay viable for the future. This requires an infusion of cash that donors are currently unable to provide. Alternatively, she is willing to explore an alliance or merger. The Board has set up a task force to assist her. She feels that its members are overly anxious and reliant on her for answers and certainty. She would like to feel more supported and to let go of her fear of failure.

Begonia's question to the group

How can I best manage this task force under such circumstances?

Group's interventions

- To what extent is the task force aware of what's in it for them if they collaborate better with you?
- What questions would you like to ask to the task force to better understand their motivations to collaborate or not?
- How can you increase your empathy for the task force members?
- What do you need to manage your own fear about the future of the organization?
- What changes do you need to make in your relationship with the Board to get more support from them?
- How do you feel about showing more vulnerability to the Board?
- How have you managed high stake situations in the past? What have you done well?
- Can you tell us what is in your control and what is not in your control?
- Is there a hidden opportunity in the crisis?

Begonia's key takeaways

- I am shifting in my perception of the challenge. I am moving outside of fear to a place of hope. I realize that I have trusted relationships on the Board I can build on. I don't have to go through this alone. I am starting to think about reinventing the organization and envisioning career opportunities for the staff
- I feel ready to open to the Board and tell them I do not have all the answers and will need their feedback
- I am rethinking how I want to engage with the task force. I want to motivate them to help me to plan our work collaboratively

Managing up

The group is a safe space to reflect on difficult relationships with bosses, Board chairs or committee chairs. Situations include managing "a difficult relationship with someone who feels threatened by me," reporting to someone "who tends to stall and lose focus," or "is not meeting the expectations of their role."

Jonquil is the President of a professional association. The relationship with the current Board Chair is not easy. Recently he gave her some feedback that she was overly combative and at time dismissive of Board members' suggestions. Jonquil's perspective is that her Board tends to overstep their boundaries of governance. She is increasingly frustrated. She feels that instead of telling her what to do, Board members should be focusing more on promoting the industry, raising their financial contribution, and streamline their decision-making process.

Jonquil's question to the group

What are my options to repair my relationship with the Board?

Group's interventions

- To what extent do you feel aligned with the Board on the association's strategy?
- What would be the benefit of a back-to-basic conversation with the Board Chair about your respective roles and responsibilities?
- Why did the Board hire you? What do they appreciate about you that you can give them more?
- How could you embrace the Board members' good intentions and offer them support?
- Is this time for a listening tour of the Board members?
- What is most draining in your working relationship with the Board? Is there a way you could delegate some of the most draining duties?
- Who are your allies on the Board?
- How can you make your Board Chair feel less threatened by you?
- How can you shift from an adversary to an educational perspective?

Jonquil's key takeaways

- I am not using my strengths as a team builder and leader to manage my relationship with the Board
- I will take the feedback and focus on the leadership development opportunity offered to me
- I will give myself space to succeed and give my Board space to succeed

Difficult people

Many members must navigate difficult relationships with peers. They seek the support of the group to reflect on "dealing with a peer's bullying behavior," "preparing for a difficult conversation with a peer who has no self-awareness," "supporting her team to manage a very difficult client." They wonder how to take care of themselves and their team when a "key stakeholder's behavior generates emotions that drain everyone," or to manage "incivilities in the workplace."

Alpina is the legal counsel of a large organization. One of her peers, a man, has a reputation of bullying his way into directing resources to the function he leads. Once again, he demands that she spares one of her direct reports for one of the projects he is leading. Alpina assertively explained her reasons to say no. The peer contacted their mutual boss to complain of her lack of cooperation. As a result, Alpina received constructive feedback from the HR lead supporting her boss, requesting that she works on her collaborative skills and work things out with this peer.

Alpina's questions to the group

Should I adjust my behavior even though I don't believe this is the right move for the organization? Should I accept to be bullied in this way? Is this a cultural norm in the company? Should I leave this company?

Group's interventions

- How can you disentangle the gender dynamics and the business issue at stake?
- What is the power of this peer? What career risks are you taking if you stand up to him?
- How can you provide valuable support and advice to this peer?
- How do you know that he is aware of his impact on you and other peers?

Additional information provided by Alpina

I am worried that I am being side-lined in favor of men. It seems that projects that should be under my realm are assigned to men on the team. I am rarely asked to contribute even though I am the legal expert.

Additional interventions from the group

- Whom can you trust?
- Who are your potential allies?
- Who on the team would lose out if you were to leave the company?
- What can you offer to them?
- How can you increase your visibility in the company?
- How can you manage your impatience while you are building your share of voice in the company?
- How comfortable are you to ask for help?

Alpina's key takeaways

- I am amazed by the ideas and insights I received from this conversation
- I will take a step back and work on fostering key relationships
- I will put time and patience into it
- In the longer term, I will consider leaving the organization if I am not able to increase my share of voice

Relationships

Women leaders aspire to better manage and generate more supportive relationships. They sometimes invite other members to help them think about novel ways to bring stronger psychological safety within their teams, to prioritize important relationships, to terminate a toxic working relationship or to develop more personal connections with co-workers.

Japhette has just been promoted to the Executive Director role of a not-for-profit organization. She has been compiling a list of quick wins to establish herself in the role and develop crucial relationships.

Japhette's question to the group

A sounding board to ensure that I have not forgotten anything for a successful on-boarding of key working relationships in my new role

Group's interventions

- What needs to evolve in your relationships with your former peers?
- What is your understanding of your team members' challenges?
- What shifts need to happen in the team's dynamics?
- Who are the insiders and influencers in the organization you need to speak to?
- Who else needs to be on your listening tour?
- How will you build trusting relationships with the Board Chair?
- Who in your network can give you guidance? Any mentors who have been through the same transition? Could your former boss play this role?
- Several group members wonder if their is a budget for Japhette to hire an on-boarding coach

Japhette's key takeaways

- I feel validated
- I was reminded on including everyone in my listening tour, regardless of their level, who has influence in this organization
- I am committed to deepening my listening skills, as if I was joining a new organization

Visibility

Occasionally, a group member will bring a visibility issue to the group, often due to the behavior of their CEO or a powerful peer who are keeping her out of strategic conversations.

Banksia's fellow executive team members operate from different countries around the world. Travel is discouraged in favor of online meetings. Banksia is not sure that she is visible and heard enough on the executive team. She has noticed that she is rarely sought after, and rarely interacts meaningfully with her peers.

Banksia's question to the group

What am I not thinking about to be more visible and sought after on the executive team?

Group's interventions

- Since everybody on the executive team is dispersed geographically, what makes you think that you are less visible than others?
- What communications are happening online outside of the executive team meetings?
- How well do people know you? Do they know your story? If you were launching a marketing campaign for yourself, how would you go about it?
- Who are the most important people you need to communicate more with?
- What assumptions might people be making about you that prevents them from reaching out?
- What have you done successfully when networking externally that is transferrable to networking internally?
- What transversal projects could you claim for yourself that would make the CEO look good?
- How can you leverage other internal networks you are connected to inside or outside of the organization?

Banksia's key takeaways

- I feel that I have a roadmap
- I feel relieved
- I am grateful for the multiple perspectives

Influence

Members will from time to time use the group to brainstorm an influence project, and or reflect on their next move in a difficult negotiation.

Fleur is the Chief Marketing Officer of a mid-cap. She is concerned about the lack of teamwork and effective decision making on the executive team. The CEO tends to offer lofty goals and to stall when making important decisions. The executive team struggles to define and sequence clear priorities. Fleur decides to call her mentor who is close to the Board. Her mentor informs her that the Board members share her concern about the CEO ability. According to Fleur's mentor, the Board worries that the CEO's lacklustre performance might impact their own ability to raise a second round of funding. After the conversation, Fleur feels increasingly frustrated.

Fleur's question to the group

How can I exert my influence to improve our decision-making process?

Group's interventions

- To what extent is the CEO aware of the situation?
- To what extent is the executive team aligned on a vision for the future?
- Which executive team members contribute the most to the team's dysfunction?
- Who agrees with you about the situation? What conversations could you have with them?
- Who is best positioned to facilitate a discussion about what it is going to take to reach the vision?
- What would it take for you to own this role? How can you leverage your position as the voice of the client? How can you connect the customer's journey with the company's priorities?
- Can you recall a situation when the team decision making went well? Could you invite the CEO to model this, using a Best Day approach?
- Would the team be more effective if some decisions were delegated to a smaller set of C-Suite executives?

Fleur's key takeaways

- Your questions have helped me clarify the issue I have
- I appreciated the balance between open-ended questions and advice
- I realize there are many avenues to try before I give up on this company
- I appreciate the nudge to play my role fully as a Chief Marketing Officer

Diversity, Equity, and Inclusion (DEI)

Women leaders in my groups are committed to elevate DEI in their organization. They sometimes ask the group to act as a sounding board as they reflect on the challenges they encounter.

Delphine is a Regional Director for an international organization. Six months ago, Delphine hired Erica on her direct team. Erica is the first and only Black woman ever hired at this level in the organization. Erica has been very successful in all her previous roles, but she is struggling to build trust and strong working relationships in this new role. She comes across as closed, does not share much about herself, and does not seem to be receptive to feedback. Delphine suggested an on-boarding coach, but Erica refused. There is increasing impatience within Delphine's team. Delphine feels guilty that she has not done enough to support Erica.

Delphine's question to the group

How can I unlock Erica's talent?

Group's interventions

- There are two Black women leaders in Delphine's group. They share their experience onboarding a new executive role. They surface unpleasant experiences, including feeling patronized at the start, having difficulties opening up to others. At the time, they questioned whether their peers were supportive or not, and tended to be defensive when receiving feedback from them. They had to work on letting go of "the chip on their shoulder." They both suggest that Delphine engages in deep conversations with Erica to break the ice.
- What is your organization's tolerance for redemption? Is there a path to give Erica space to "rebrand" herself while managing her peers' impatience? What conversations can you plan with Erica's peers?
- How comfortable do you feel about coaching Erica to increase her confidence to share more about herself?

- Since Erica has refused a coach, how comfortable would she be debriefing a 360 report with HR?
- What lessons have you learned from this experience? What is this situation asking you to do as a leader?
- What is the perspective of Erica's team? What are the benefits of step meetings with members of her team?
- Who can help you best prepare for these conversations within your organization?

Delphine's key takeaways

- I feel relieved and grateful that I could talk openly with you without feeling judged
- I love the concept of redeeming and I am committed to supporting Erica in her journey
- I will seek help from the organization. I don't have to do this alone

Feedback

Women leaders regret that they are not receiving enough actionable feedback in their organizations. At the same time, they struggle to process the feedback they receive, and find it difficult to give feedback to others.

Gyp is on the C-Suite of a company that has recently been acquired. Her new boss has promoted her to a larger role in which she will supervise some of her former peers. Before taking her new role, she takes a short vacation. During that time her boss receives negative feedback about her management style from her former peers. Upon her return he changed his mind and asked Gyp to start as an interim in the role. He will then promote her once she demonstrates her ability to address the feedback he received. Gyp is shocked by the process and feels that the feedback is untrue and unfair. She accepts to start as an interim but her heart is not in it.

Gyp's question to the group

I would like to get your perspective on the situation to help me think about my next move

Group's interventions

- What is your take on the culture of the acquiring company?
- What felt relevant in the feedback that you received when you came back from leave?
- Your need an alignment conversation with your boss. How can you best prepare for it?
- If you make a conscious, dispassionate assessment of the role that is proposed to you, how much of a fit is it with your career objectives?
- What other information do you need, and from whom, to decide what your next move should be?
- What needs have been surfaced by the feedback that you could address?
- What will you prove to yourself if you stick to this role?
- How can you disentangle your professional identity from the feedback you have received in this new company?
- Through this feedback, what are you learning about the company? Is this a good fit for you?
- What are the leadership development opportunities for you in this role?

Gyp's key takeaways

- I need to take time to regroup and to give myself grace. I am taking this feedback too personally
- I am ready to go with the flow and make the most of the situation while I consider my next move

Why women leaders leave a group

This is what I have learned from the exit and entry interviews that I have conducted with transitioning members.

If there is a curation error, women leaders will quickly determine that their challenges and opportunities do not match that of the rest of the group and ask to leave.

Likewise, they will not stay in a group that does not develop a strong connection. They will be particularly susceptible to individual disrupting behaviors that are not being addressed by the group coach. For instance, they will cite "a member who was taking all the space and talking too much during the sessions," "members who did not attend most of the sessions," "members who never arrive on time, or leave before the end of the session."

When cohesion is strong, it is rare that members leave because of the other group members. However, I have heard members report feeling "rushed," "unfinished," needing a "deeper dive," or "more time for this." When exploring further, we have almost always agreed that the group experience was not a good fit with the depth at which they needed to go to address an overwhelming personal challenge and that they would be better served by individual coaching.

In a high-functioning group, the main reason for departure is the loss of sponsorship. In other instances, a member decides to allocate their leadership development budget differently to meet an emerging leadership need (for example: on-boarding to a new role). Most women leaders prefer to be sponsored rather than spending out of pocket, because they tend to prioritize their loved ones over themselves when spending their own money. When they are sponsored, they are they are very conscious of how much money the organization is spending on them and tend to err on the conversative side: "I cannot possibly ask my boss for both executive coaching and group coaching."

The next most important reason to leave a group is a change of personal circumstances that makes attendance to the group session impossible (for instance, a monthly Board meeting that is suddenly scheduled at the same date or a relocation to an incompatible time zone).

Sometimes, their current group becomes less meaningful for their own leadership development due to a shift in their career (retiring, leave of absence, transition to a different category of leadership).

Finally, women leaders will tend to leave when the group dips below five members, because there is less cross-fertilization.

Reflective questions about Chapter 2

- What are the benefits of looking at your practice from a systems perspective?
- What surprised you when reviewing the hopes and expectations of women leaders when they start group coaching?
- What similarities and differences do you see between the benefits experienced by women leaders in one-on-one executive coaching and the benefits reported in this chapter?
- What themes brought by women leaders seem unique to their gender? How might this inform their experience of group coaching?

- When reading the small case studies, to what extent did you relate to their challenge as a person and as a practitioner? How might that inform your approach as a group coach?
- What do you make of the reasons why women leaders leave coaching?
- What other reflections and questions came up after reading this chapter?

Bibliography

Florent-Treacy, E. (2009). Behind the scenes in the identity laboratory: Participant's narratives of identity transition through group coaching in a leadership development programme. *International Coaching Psychology Review*, *4*(1), 71–86.

Gray, D., De Haan, E., & Bonneywell, S. (2019). Coaching the 'ideal worker': Female leaders and the gendered self in a global corporation. *European Journal of Training and Development*, *43*(7/8), 661–681.

Schalk, M., & Landeta, J. (2017). Internal versus external executive coaching. *Coaching: An International Journal of Theory, Research and Practice*, *10*(2), 140–156.

Tuckman, B. W. (1965). Developmental sequence in small groups. *Psychological Bulletin*, *63*(6), 384.

Tuckman, B. W., & Jensen, M. A. C. (1977). Stages of small-group development revisited. *Group & Organization Studies*, *2*(4), 419–427.

Chapter 3

Forming a Coaching Group with Women Leaders

Key points of Chapter 3

✓ Because the quality of curation is the first reason why members stay or leave, the composition of the group must be balanced carefully between similarities that will strengthen cohesion and diversities that will enhance creativity.

✓ Ground rules need to be realistic and clearly related to the performance of the group.

✓ A fully formed group is cohesive and psychologically safe. The role of the group coach is to foster practices that will improve both. Storytelling, inclusion, openness to questions, acceptance of failure, invitation to contribute, openness to challenge, consistency and transparency are the most important practices.

Purpose of Chapter 3

Priya Parker, in her book, *The Art of Gathering* (2020), suggests that her "job is to put the right people in a room and help them collectively think, dream, argue, heal, envision, trust, and connect for a specific larger purpose." This is very similar to what I think is the role of the group coach when forming a group of women leaders.

This chapter is the first of three that focuses on what a group coach thinks and does. It covers the reflexions and actions that support the forming of a group of women leaders for the purpose of mutual coaching. The chapter starts by covering best practices in curating the group. It continues with important ground rules to discuss with the group. Next, I cover how to foster cohesion in the group, which is not only considered as a key benefit by women leaders, but it also foundational to the generation of new insights.

DOI: 10.4324/9781003465195-4

Then, I consider the importance of a consistent experience for the group members and propose a structure to a group coaching session. The chapter ends with various tips and techniques that I have picked up over the years to increase cohesion in a group.

Curation

Inadequate curation is the first reason that women leaders give for leaving a coaching group. When a group member feels that they can't help other members or can't get help from them, they quickly disengage.

How many members in a group?

There is no research that has assessed group size as a moderator of performance in group coaching. Group psychotherapy research suggests that the optimal group size varies between five and ten. The review of group coaching models in Chapter 1 (Table 1.3) indicates that most researchers have used groups of five to eight participants. As a practitioner, I have worked with groups between 4 and 12 participants with equal success. There is a consensus in group dynamics research that group size is inversely related to group cohesion. Indeed, the larger the group, the more difficult it is to read nonverbal cues and group dynamics. However, group size is positively related to group insight generation. In addition, the capacity of the group leader to manage complex group dynamics is positively related to the performance of larger groups.

Minimize conflicting loyalties

It is obvious that conflicts of interest must be eliminated in the curation of a group. It is not possible for a group to function well when several members are legally restricted in what they can share with each other. Conflicting loyalties between group members or between a group member and a group coach are not illegal but they are ill advised, since they cause ethical dilemmas for the parties involved and adversely impact the cohesion of the group.

To minimize the risk of conflicting loyalties, once you have checked for conflicts of interest, select members who work in different organizations, different industries, and different supply chains. With social media engines such as LinkedIn, it is possible to view whether they are connected. In addition, select women leaders you do not know. Do not include a group member whom you know as a friend, neighbour, family member or colleague. Avoid including in your group someone whom you have individually coached, or who is currently a client in any capacity.

Maximize alignment

Alignment is a major component of cohesion. Ensure that the prospective members' learning objectives, and hopes are aligned with the conditions and expected benefits of group coaching.

To achieve alignment, I recommend a questionnaire completed by a one-on-one call with each prospective member. Craft questions that will allow you to detect whether the woman leader is a good fit for the group. If you can, help participants decide whether group coaching is really the best option for them, particularly in the following situations:

- their present circumstances are not a good fit for regular attendance to group work
- their learning style is not a good fit for group work
- their learning objectives are technical or functional
- they need a deep dive in a particular leadership topic (job transition, investors' relation, etc.)

A group member was looking for something else

During our first group coaching session, Salix, a recently promoted CMO, shared her objective to learn more about the day-to-day job of different functional leads to perform better in her role. She then expressed concerns that there might not be enough deep functional expertise in the group. When I prompted her to share what she wanted to offer to the group, she said that she was not sure. I thanked her for her contribution, and we heard from another member. After the group meeting, I asked for a few minutes of her time one on one, so that we could debrief her first impressions. During this conversation, we established that group coaching was not the best solution for her, and that she engages instead in mentoring or training.

Manage diversity

Maximizing cohesion and insight generation through curating is akin to managing a polarity. The more similar the group members, the more likely they will bond quickly. In contrast, the more diverse the group, the more varied input members will receive.

There are four dimensions in which similarity is more productive than diversity.

- mastery of the language used in the group
- level in the organization
- scope of responsibility
- life stage

Heterogenous levels of mastery of the group language will make it difficult for the group coach offer a pace that will work for everyone. In general, the level of language mastery dictates the level of nuance with which challenges and opportunities will be discussed. When the level of language mastery is low to moderate, I recommend using more individual reflective moments. I also suggest relying more on visual or kinaesthetic techniques.

Differences in group members' career stages and life stages will surface mentoring needs or reverse mentoring offers, that are best addressed in a one-on-one space. Arguably, top-level management women leaders are already mentoring younger women or receiving reverse mentoring from their younger team members. This is not what group coaching is about.

In contrast, when the group coach and the group members embrace inclusive practices, a diversity of personal and social identities will benefit the generation of insights for group members. Indeed, research on the quality of decision-making shows that diverse teams make better decisions than individuals 87% of the time, compared to non-diverse teams who make better decisions that individuals 66% of the time. While diversity can increase friction in a group by 15%, inclusive practices will increase decision-making quality by 60%. If possible, avoid having only one representative of a given social identity in your group. If this is not feasible, be explicit about the situation with the prospective group member so that they can make an informed decision. Remind them that there is always a risk that they become an "only" at a later stage in the life of the group if its composition changes.

Ground rules

Once members have enrolled in group coaching, many will still be unclear about the process. Shared ground rules are fundamental to align hopes and expected results of a group coaching intervention. Ground rules need to be realistic, clearly related to group performance, understood, agreed upon, experimented with, and revisited as needed throughout the group's life.

Offer realistic ground rules

Women leaders are generally overcommitted and often the first go-to person if there is a family or business emergency. Ensure that your ground rules are supportive of the multiple roles they play.

Women leaders are more likely than other to be expected to attend to emergencies. As a result, I do not request mandatory attendance to group meetings.

Because of their busy schedule, it is unrealistic to expect that all group members will read or view some material before a session. As a result, I never assign any reading in advance. Instead, supporting material can be offered after a session for group members who want to commit more time to reflect on their own.

Do not assume that group members will remember ground rules

Typically, proposed ground rules are shared verbally during the one-on-ones with prospective members before and after their first meeting. In addition, I strongly recommend creating orientation material. You can't expect that they are read, but at least you can refer to them.

As we will see in Chapter 5, each time you notice a dysfunctional behavior with a member or with the group, it is an opportunity to revisit the ground rules.

I have found that taking time out of the first meeting to introduce ground rules in relation to the performance of the group is the most effective way to help members internalize them.

Relate the ground rules to the performance of the group

Remind group members that the two most important indicators of a high functioning group are cohesion and the generation of new insights for all members. Review each ground rule in relation to each indicator.

Ground rules that support cohesion

1) Alignment about the scope of group coaching
   Especially if members have not volunteered to participate in the intervention, articulate the purpose of group coaching by sharing its definition and expected benefits

   - Explain the role of the group coach, highlighting the differences between a group coach and a dyadic coach, a facilitator, or a trainer. Remind members that the group coach cannot individually coach them. Gently yet firmly remind boundaries when a member asks you for one-on-one spot coaching between group coaching sessions.
   - Remind members whom to contact for what questions, especially if you are contracted by a coaching service provider.

- Define what can and cannot be brought to group coaching
  - leadership topics rather than technical or functional topics
  - coaching issues rather than psychotherapeutic issues
  - strategic questions rather than tactical questions

Asking for tactical support

Some group members, especially if they belong to a peer advisory group, are used to asking for and offering tactical support. Example of tactical support include giving your tactical opinion, offering introductions or recommendations.

In my groups we agree that tactical topics will be addressed directly between interested parties, in-between sessions. When a need for tactical advice surfaces during group coaching, the members involved commit to a space and time to discuss one-on-one after the session.

2) Consistent attendance

Strong attendance is very important during the first four meetings, because it will build the bonding and cohesion of the group. The smaller your group, the stronger the impact of a member's absence on group cohesion. The group coach can increase attendance by giving advanced, repeated, and clear communication of the schedule, duration, and location of group coaching sessions.

Protocols for late arrivals and early departures from a session are another ground rule to discuss in relation to the cohesion of the group. You can minimize the disruption if you request that the group member informs you in advance. My groups generally agree that the late arriving member waits to speak until invited to do so, and that the early departing member does not present her challenge/opportunity that day in case there is not enough time for completion of the process.

Members coming in and out of the session

At the start of my group coaching career, I worked from Jakarta, Indonesia, where traffic was so bad that the commuting times were unpredictable. We quickly realized that we could not start nor end at reliable times. In addition, we had to accept that members drop in and out of sessions to respond to urgent calls due of the complexity of coordinating calendars. It became so difficult to manage that we decide to discontinue group coaching format in favour of an open space approach which embraces members coming in and out of the reflective space.

I was confronted to the same challenge again more recently when all meetings shifted online at the start of the Covid Pandemic. Some members had to drop in out of our meetings to take care of home-schooled children, take urgent calls from work, etc. The fact that I had more experience by then did not make things any easier. Nowadays we agree with group members to abstain from this unless they face a personal emergency (dropping children at the bus stop when a caregiver is delayed counts as one, of course!).

3) Confidentiality

Confidentiality is a core foundation of trust and psychological safety within the group. It's a rule that is easily understood by everyone. However, it will compete with loyalty if members know each other separately from the group, leading to tortuous dilemmas for the member. The more you minimize the likelihood of competing loyalties in the curation of the group, the less risk you have that cohesion will be compromised, and confidentiality broken.

4) Manage expectations about the group composition.

It's best to set expectations to prospective members at the start of the group that the group composition might evolve over time. There are several reasons for this. Curation is not always spot on the first time. The perception of fit may evolve over time. Some members must leave due to external circumstances (moving to another time zone is a frequent one). To maintain a suitable size for the group, it is possible to bring in a new member or a small group of new members from time to time. I would advise not to do it too frequently for the sake of protecting the group cohesion.

Ground rules that support the generation of new insights

1) Horizontal feedback

Horizontal feedback happens when a member gives feedback to another member. It is an important benefit of group coaching. However, most women leaders have a difficult relationship with feedback, which they often perceive as disingenuous in the workplace. As one member reflected: "I realize there is no real feedback in my company, and I need other sources of feedback."

To train the muscle of feedback within the group from a safe perspective, it's a good idea to start with appreciative feedback. Members evoke the benefits of positive feedback in such terms as: "positive feedback keeps me motivated," "I experienced and appreciate the power of positive feedback," I reassess how I am looking at myself," "I was so focused on my story's outcome, I did not realize the positives in the journey." Once cohesion and mutual trust is well established, members will often request both positive and constructive feedback from other members. Here is how they experience more constructive feedback from the group: "feedback is a gift when given with positive intent," "[when I presented my issue], I got feedback that completely challenged what I was expecting to hear," "I feel pushed and kicked in the ass," "receiving feedback in a safe space, the group called me out and woke me up," "we are not afraid to give each other feedback."

I recommend using appreciative inquiry as soon as possible in the group to get them acclimated to feedback progressively and safely. Typically, in the third session, members start remembering their mutual backgrounds. This model works in two phases. In phase one, the presenter shares an important formative experience as a leader. Group members listen while consulting a handout containing a list of generic strengths. At the end of the story each group member tells the presenter which strengths they have heard. Then, the presenter shares their key-takeaway. In phase two, the presenter shares a current leadership challenge. Presenter and group members brainstorm on ways the presenter could use the strengths surfaced in phase one to address the challenge.

In the example shown in Table 3.1 below, group members who have been together for one year invite Daisy to reflect on her strengths and in what ways she might have underused them or overused them. The feedback is based on the issues Daisy brought to the group and the reactions, insights, and questions she has offered when supporting other members.

2) Vertical feedback

The group coach role plays an important role fostering a climate of safety in feedback by modelling the practice. In this example, I ask a question at the start of a session: "What was the most joyful moment of your week and why?". I am met with dead silence. After what feels like an eternity (but is really about 30 seconds) I ask another question: "From your perspective, what does this silence mean?". After another silence, one member responds: "there is so much despair right now, so much suffering in the world, I don't see how I can possibly be joyful". I thank the member

Table 3.1 An example of appreciative inquiry during a group coaching session

Strengths shared by group members	Daisy's reflections
A risk-taker to get to what you strive to	Overused. Risk of being perceived as impatient
Not afraid of failure	Well-used. Has allowed me to grow
A broad experience to share	Underused. I need to increase my share of voice
Bold	Overused. May put people off
Charismatic	Well-used. I make the best of my speaking engagements
Expressive	Overused. Sometimes it's useful to not respond too quicky
Passionate	Underused. I don't use this enough as a compass
Innovative and creative with your career	Well used. Has allowed me to rebound in my career
Compassionate, gracious, and generous	Well-used. Has allowed me to develop life-long relationships
Strategic	Under-used, for myself. Well-used in my professional roles

for her contribution, and I ask other group members how her response lands on them. A few members admit that had also felt some guilt about my original question. I ask: "what would be a better question?". One member volunteers: "If I did not feel guilty, what would I share?". The other members are now nodding in unison, giving permission to each group member to answer my original question in a way that works for them.

If you want group members to give you effective feedback, you must use a common vocabulary. Therefore, it is very important to communicate your role very clearly at the start of the group coaching journey and to be explicit about what you are doing, from time to time. For instance, members should not expect you to be an active participant while a presenter discusses a challenge or opportunity with the group. However, if you do intervene, ask for permission, and explain why.

Tell the members to expect process checks from time to time and do them! In my practice, this is the only way I know to find out if I am setting the right pace for the group coaching process. Do not assume that you have the magical ability to sense it. You might have missed non-verbal cues, especially when you have a large group on video. Check with the group what the experience is. For example, it might seem that a group might have run out of questions for a presenter because there is a silence. Check with the known introverts in the group if they have something to add. Then check again. Then ask the presenter what their key takeaways are, and if they feel complete. One thing that I often hear is "I don't want to take up all the time." In fact, it can be useful for the group to go deeper especially when the topic is likely to resonate with all the group members.

3) Basic coaching skills

Most senior women leaders are already very effective at coaching their team members. However, the group coach should review basic coaching skills with members, including deep listening (listening for facts, emotions, and values), active listening (summaries, paraphrasing, and checking for mutual understanding), suspension of judgement, open-ended questions, and storytelling. If you are going to use a specific coaching model, teach it first and then use it consistently.

The consistent use of coaching skills will strengthen cohesion and the generation of new insights for members. We will review these techniques in detail in the next chapter.

Cohesion and psychological safety

In the forming phase of the group, the key task of the coach is to support the development of cohesion. In group dynamics theory, cohesion is defined as a group's degree of unity. Forsyth (2021) describes cohesion through multiple dimensions: attraction to the group, commitment to the group, importance of the group for each member, social identification with the group, shared emotional experiences, stable group structure, and the display of common features during group interactions.

Research in group psychotherapy has surfaced that cohesion, and especially horizontal cohesion, is foundational to the generation of new insights for each individual member for two main reasons:

- it is the conduit to psychological safety, which allows each member to trust the group and empowers them to share
- it strengthens social influence, the process by which a group member changes their beliefs or behaviors because of their interactions with other group members

As described in the previous section of the chapter, the establishment and frequent communication of shared ground rules will go a long way to ensuring cohesion. However, ground rules, while necessary, are not a sufficient condition to group cohesion.

Storytelling

To form a cohesive group, members need to know each other well, so that they can appreciate what they have in common, as a well as the diverse values, experiences, and communication styles that exist in the group and how they contribute to the group's success.

Mutual interpersonal trust is paramount to the success of a group. Even after the ground rules are shared and mutually agreed upon, anxiety will linger. Participants will be apprehensive of being exposed. This is especially true for women leaders who must navigate a fine line between being authentic and being seen as meeting the patriarchal standards of leadership. Trust is the belief that each group member is competent, reliable, and benevolent to let them take interpersonal risks. As each group member gets to know other members more deeply, more information and observations will be collected about each participant's traits. As trust grows it will be easier to take the risk to disclose personal and professional leadership challenges that might not have been shared with anyone yet. It will also lower defensiveness when members air differences of opinions or share difficult feedback. Such level of vulnerability is foundational to transformational learning.

What group members say about storytelling

"a space where I don't feel isolated," "a sense of tribe," "a realization that we can learn from each other," "I feel understood in the challenges I am facing in my role," "I admire the other group members," "it renews the sisterhood spirit," "there is power in collective story telling."

Stories promote deeper mutual understanding and a greater sense of universality. They can be used at the start of the group coaching journey to help members better understand each other. Ongoingly, they help create psychological safety in cultures where the experience of shame is socially undesirable. Finally, they are extremely useful to generate new insights.

The importance of managing storytelling time

Story telling is a powerful catalyst of bonding in the group. Therefore, my first sessions are always about story telling. Depending on the number of participants and the duration of the session, you will need to think carefully about the reflective exercise you want to use. It is fundamental that every member gets a chance to tell their story. At the same time, at the end of each story, some space needs to be carved out for one or two members to share a comment or a question. As a result, time management is critical. As in every group, members will place themselves on a continuum between high extroversion and high introversion. Before starting the story-telling exercise, I normalize the situation, reminding everyone that extroverts need to talk in order to think and introverts need to think in order to talk. I invite extroverts to work as hard as they can to be concise. I remind introverts that there will be a reflection period before we start and invite them to share their input even if they deem it as incomplete. I also announce that there is a finite time for each member and that I will need to interrupt the presentation that goes over so that everyone can get a turn.

Psychological safety

Psychological safety is the shared belief that the group is safe for interpersonal risk-taking. It is the equivalent of having trust in the group you belong to. It is fundamental that the experience of psychological safety is discussed in the group and that members can define how to measure it.

Members share the markers of psychological safety in one of my groups

- consensual group coaching process
- emphasis on leveraging diversity of styles and perspectives
- appreciating when fresh perspectives are brought into the discussion
- noticing when new ideas are triggered
- emphasizing the learning process rather than the result
- being comfortable when our contributions fall flat
- there is no need to always provide the right answer
- expressing gratitude for the space

Managing psychological safety in international groups

Intercultural awareness is also important to understand and manage the group dynamics. If personality were hardware, culture would be software. Multicultural studies inform us that an extroverted British person may sound like an introverted Mediterranean. Or that an optimistic French may sound like a cautiously pessimistic American, etc. In addition, some cultures are more communal than individualistic. Some are more deferent than others. Some are more contextual than task oriented. If your group is multinational, it can be helpful to invite them to share about the surprises they encountered living or working in a different country from their own. This book is not the place to give you a comprehensive understanding of intercultural issues. Even if you are well travelled and have lived in different countries, do not assume that you know and do not make assumptions.

The four levels of psychological safety

Both the curation of the group and its ground rules are extremely important to create the conditions for psychological safety. However, these are not sufficient conditions. The group coach needs to model and encourage group members to strengthen psychological safety throughout the group's journey.

According to Timothy Clark, there are four stages of psychological safety that build on each other: inclusion, learning, contribution, and challenge, as show on Figure 3.1 below.

1) Inclusion: safe to be who you are

It's useful to remind ourselves what inclusion is and what it is not. Inclusion is a set of behaviors that signal that it is permissible to be authentic during the group coaching process (if you don't break the ground rules). It is different from diversity, which is factual. It is different from belonging, which is a feeling, and it is different from equity, which is an ideal. It is the role of the coach to model inclusive behaviors and to advocate for them.

CHALLENGE
safe to ask
for a change

CONTRIBUTION
safe to add

LEARNING
safe to ask and to fail

INCLUSION
safe to be who you are

Figure 3.1 The four levels of psychological safety.

The first inclusive behavior is storytelling (again). To promote an inclusive environment at the start of the intervention, the group coach should ensure that group members have an opportunity to hear how each member experience their identities.

The second inclusive behavior is appreciative inquiry. This means asking questions about the qualities and strengths that are at play in any given situation narrated by a member. Appreciative questions include "what worked well?", "what is already in place?", "what strengths have you deployed?", "what strengths are applicable?".

The third inclusive behavior is share of voice. To promote inclusion and contribution, the group coach ensures that each member has an equal opportunity to share and gently challenge some of the quieter members to speak up, and some of the more talkative members to speak less. The group coach also ensures that each member has an equal opportunity to receive group coaching from others. Keeping track of who received coaching when is therefore very important.

The fourth inclusive behavior is constructive feedback. The group should model the way by providing behavioral feedback to the group members and asking for behavioral feedback from the group members.

Many women leaders have mastered inclusive behaviors, because they know how it feels without them. They had to build their professional identities in environments where their authentic strengths are underappreciated and underutilized. In addition, they are on the receiving end of microaggressions that undermine their psychological safety at work, leading them to tone down or hide important parts of their identity.

In addition, women leaders are twice as likely as men to spend time on Diversity Equity and Inclusion initiatives in addition to their regular work duties. They are more collaborative with their teams and more likely to promote inclusive behavior. As a result, they possess deep knowledge and practice about inclusive behaviors.

Promoting inclusion in an international group of women leaders

These women leaders are employed by the same international organization. They have arrived from different countries to attend their first group coaching session as part of an international women leadership development program. After mutual introductions, I invite them to share how their nationalities have shaped them as leaders. Here are a few examples:

"If I think about what shaped me most a child, it is my status as an immigrant. I grew up with no sense of entitlement. I was the first in my family to go to high-school and to the university and even earn a Masters' degree. This made me a life-long learner."

"I grew up in a traditional, catholic family. When I realized I was gay, it took me decades to share it with my mother. During that time, even the most difficult conversation felt so easy in comparison! All these years, everyone thought of me an outstanding communicator and influencer…but that's really not the case!"

"I come from South-East Asia. We emigrated to Australia so that I could complete my university degree. I became the first graduate in my family. For my parents, I was defined as a ROI. I studied really hard to meet their expectations. When I was rejected from an honour's program, I experienced a lot of shame and worked even harder to get into a PhD program. Since then, I am always running, asking myself what else can I do to excel?"

"I am an Indian expatriate. My mother is not in good health, and I am the elder daughter. Each time there is a health scare, I am expected to drop everything and fly back home to care for her, often for weeks at a time. Once there, I work and parent online at night and take care of my mother during the day. This has really strengthened my resilience and how I manage my energy."

"In my country of origin, homosexuality is a crime. When I came out to my parents who still live there, they were angry and terrified. Since then, I keep proving myself to my family, I make personal sacrifices and stretches myself thin by providing care and money to family members who are in need."

"I was born and raised in a South American dictatorship. This has profoundly influenced how I views psychological safety as a foundation of leadership. I have a regular gratitude practice since I moved to a Western democracy."

"I come from a poor East-European country, and I speak English with a strong accent. Since moving here, I am truly rooting for the underdog. This value sits at the core of my leadership brand. At the same time, my citizenship and especially my accent feeds my impostor syndrome".

"I moved to South Asia with my parents when I was a young child. I have always felt like an outsider both in my country of origin as well as in my country of adoption. I think this has impacted my ability to form trusting relationships quickly with work colleagues".

"As a teenager, I emigrated with my parents from a troubled Middle Eastern country. I felt ostracized at school. This made me more introverted and more undecisive that I would like to be. Sometimes, I wonder if this has impacted my career trajectory".

When I ask participants to share their key takeaways, here are some reactions:

"I am inspired to better understand how my team members identity is shaped by the culture of their country of origin. I would like to go through the same exercise with my team."

"I am more acutely aware of how privileged my heterosexual identity is."

"I am revisiting how I engage with my Eastern European colleagues: have I been too arrogant with them?"

"There are so many blessings that we take for granted. I am inspired to engage in a gratitude practice."

Immigrant or expatriate women leaders must navigate different family and work cultural norms. Some may feel excluded from conversations because of their lack of knowledge of the popular culture of the host country. For example, as a French immigrant to the United States, I can't relate to baseball metaphors. When I lived in Asia as an expatriate, I was often reminded that individual achievement was a Western concept, while many Asians were more committed to communal welfare.

Women with disabilities experience a combination of gender and ableist stereotypes. Their competence is more often challenged than other women. I once lead a group online, that included a self-described, visually impaired member. Through her highly valuable contribution to the group process, she was instrumental in helping other women in the group navigate their own stereotypes.

In the United States, at the intersection of race and gender, while inclusion research and training opportunities are increasing, little change has been experienced for women leaders from non-White ethnicities. In fact, research shows that Black, Latinas, and Asian-American women leaders are more likely than White women leaders to be the main bread winner, to shoulder a greater share of the care giving responsibilities, and to be expected to excel in all categories. Outside of the United States, the experience of a non-White ethnicity can be fundamentally different. In one of my groups, a black Nigerian expatriate to the United States was shocked to see how her self-concept and previous experience of psychological safety were different from black Americans. Since working in the US, she was struggling to manage her interactions with White men leaders in her organization. The perspective of black American women in the group helped her illuminate the barriers at play.

LGBTQ+ leaders, in countries where they are allowed to come out, are more often than others expected to dress with clothing that is aligned with their biological gender. In one of my groups, a lesbian member who typically dresses as a man was once asked to participate in a panel of women leaders to discuss executive presence. The panel organizer suggested that women facilitators wear "power dresses" to model the way. She politely declined.

2) Learning: safe to ask questions and safe to fail

As we have seen in the first chapter, women leaders are extremely wary of failing because of the double bind effect they must navigate in organizations. They are also often thrown into crisis jobs under the false assumption that they are less likely to fail than men. In the example below, Cosmos seeks the help of the group to mitigate the risk of failure:

Cosmos, a Chief Strategy Officer, is the only C-Suite employee left from her former business line after it was combined into another. The CEO of the combined business line has a centric view of leadership. As a result, his executive team is perceived as less collaborative than in other business units. The CEO reluctantly hired Cosmos after being challenged by his boss to change the culture of his team. Cosmos is worried that she has been set up for failure.

Cosmos question to the group

What is my path to success in this role?

Group's interventions

- How can you gain the trust of your peers?
- Since the boss hand-picked you, is there a path for you to become his confidante?
- Who are your allies in the recombined business unit? How can you activate them for support?
- What are your boss strengths that you could leverage in your role?
- What else do you need to ask to better understand the situation?

Cosmos key takeaways

- I have a roadmap
- I feel more confident

Additionally, in some Asian, Middle Eastern and African cultures, failure is conflated with shame. An individual will do anything to avoid feeling ashamed and everything possible to avoid that others around them feel shame. This aversion to shame makes it very difficult to ask questions. Indeed, you could feel ashamed if it turns out that you should have known the answer. You could put someone to shame if you asked a question that offended them or that they could not answer. In addition, shame makes it very uncomfortable to share failures or to hear someone else tell a story of failure. It also makes them adverse to giving or receiving any constructive feedback.

The group coach needs to assess quickly how women leaders feel about failure and shame in the group and ensure that they are treated with respect. There are other ways to create learning that to reflect on past failures. As I mentioned earlier in the chapter, appreciative inquiry works very well to foster learning. To test the tolerance of group members for failure, I often invite members to share a short story: "when a failure became the best thing that could have happened to me," "when I shared a personal failure with a direct report to help them normalize a situation and rebound." I also ask them to reflect on "how safe is it, in their organization, to fail as a leader?".

3) Contribution: safe to share your opinion

The group must encourage each group member to actively contribute to each coaching round.

Like safety to fail, safety to share is not always a given for women leaders in their own organization. Here is an example from a group coaching session:

Clarkia, a Chief Legal Officer, is the only woman in the C-Suite of a large organization. Recently she gave expert advice to one of her peers during an executive committee meeting to help them address a business crisis. She was rebuffed by this peer even though he has no technical knowledge of the matter. Nobody came to her defence. Even though she knew that she gave the correct advice, she said she was going to double check her information. This is not the first instance that she feels underappreciated and guilty of not speaking up in the moment when challenged by one of her peers.

Clarkia's question to the group

Is there anything I could do differently to better assert myself?

Group's interventions

- Several group members shared that they had faced similar situations when giving expert advice to their peers. One group member said that when she brought the matter to the CEO, he said that she had the timing wrong. Clarkia reacted to this, noticing that her CEO gave her the following feedback: "I told you to let it go." Another group member noticed how her imposter syndrome increased when her expert advice was dismissed
- To what extent do you feel that your CEO and peer trust you?
- What impact does your expert advice have on them? Is there an emotional impact that you could address to make it easier for them to process your advice?
- How could you follow up with the CEO about his comment: "I told you to let it go"
- How would you address the issue if you knew that they feared the consequences of your advice on their own self-confidence?
- How can you stay neutral and non-judgmental as you follow-up on your advice?

Clarkia's key takeaways

- I don't feel alone with my problem anymore
- I feel a lot better about my issue
- I am ready to build my influence strategy and consider different scenarios

In addition, there are cultures that are more hierarchical than others. In these cultures, it is very difficult to challenge a person who is perceived as being in a position of authority. Sometimes, the group coach is assumed to be in the position of authority. Sometimes, it's other group members who appear to have more experience coaching others and ask "better" questions.

To mitigate for this risk, it's best to invite members who have not contributed so far if they would like to ask a question or to share a thought. If they prefer not to, I ask the question "How is the situation resonating for you?"

Boosting engagement during a round of group coaching

When a presenter is faced with silence, the group coach should help the group to engage. The best way to achieve this is to invite the group to elevate the presented topic to a group-level theme. To ensure that the transition is smooth for the presenter, I start with a quick summary of the presented topic and check with the presenter if I have correctly sized it. Once we are aligned, I ask questions to the group such as: "How does this topic resonate with you?", or "What have you learned from addressing a similar challenge?".

4) Challenge: safe to ask for change

This is the most difficult element of psychological safety to navigate. When it comes to the process of group coaching, you remain the expert. While you have to be open to feedback from members, you also have to push back constructively when members demands are not conducive to effective group coaching.

I like to use two questions to invite members to contribute to my professional development as a coach. From time to time, I ask "what is working well for you?", "what is not working well for you? Then, I am explicit that I will need time to reflect on the thoughts that have been shared. I use my reflective practice time to sort out what requests are worth experimenting with and what requests need to be respectfully challenged.

In Chapter 5, I will address how to respond to members that have a pattern of challenging you unconstructively.

My top three tips to strengthen psychological safety

- I invite the group to rediscuss the ground rules when something is no longer working. This strengthens the self-confidence of the group
- I always start my group coaching sessions with a warm-up question, because they ease members into the group coaching process and makes them feel more comfortable. Here are three of my favourites:

  - What do you most like about your neighborhood, and why? (To increase bonding)

- A joy audit: scan yesterday, last week, last month – what brought you your job and why? (To increase positive energy)
- What was the best piece of feedback you received last month? What did you learn from it? (To generate potential coaching topics)

- Equity is an important element of cohesion: therefore, I insist that group members take their turn as presenters, unless someone has a good reason to take a pass

Other important techniques to form a group

Model the way

The group coach supports the development of vertical and horizontal cohesion by embodying warmth, grace, and positivity. The facial expressions should be encouraging, smiling, nodding, mirroring as needed. I always thank a member who volunteers to start a conversation. I thank each member after they have shared a story. When I challenge a member, I do it with lightness, from a place of compassion and caring. In addition, I regularly ask permission to group members when I am planning to change from one role to the other (for instance, moving from listening to sharing).

Consistency

The role of the group coach is paramount in ensuring a consistent experience for the group.

This sounds obvious but the coach should model the way and strictly follow the rules of engagement that have been mutually agreed upon. For example, one of the most important roles of the group coach is to start on time, manage the time, and end on time.

I also invite the group coach to have a predictable structure to the group coaching, possibly offering some rituals, as shown in Table 3.2 below.

Transparency

During the meeting, moving from one phase to the next should be made explicit. Here are some of the statements I make when transitioning:

- from the beginning to the middle of the session: "it looks like we are ready to move to group coaching"
- from the middle to end of the session: "as we are approaching the end of the call, I suggest we take the time to share your key takeaways"

Table 3.2 My preferred structure for a group coaching intervention

Group coaching session stage	Timing	Content
Pre-session (3 days before)	Message group members	Agenda Logistics
Introduction	20% of meeting time	Warm up question, updates, agenda
Body	60% of meeting time	Group coaching
End	20% of meeting time	Key takeaways, date of next meeting
Post-session (day of or after)	Message group members	Summary of key takeaways Date of next meeting Information shared or promised during the previous meeting (example: a book reference, a handout, a web link, etc.)

Sharing key takeaways

The coach should invite members to share what they have learned about themselves and what they have learned about the group at least once during each session. It helps member reflect on the benefits of a collaborative atti-tude. Often my participants reflect that they have learned as much, if not more about themselves, when contributing to coach someone else in the group. The more they internalize the benefits of a collaborative attitude as opposed to a self-centred perspective, the more they will display it.

The benefits of sharing key takeaways

At the end of the first session, when I ask for key takeaways, mem-bers almost always mention feeling connected with each other, notic-ing: "the easiness with which we bonded," "a place of closeness," "witnessing the start of the bonding process," "a personal connec-tion with each of you," "so much resonated, I can't wait to dive in," "camaraderie, easy bounding, a safe place already, I feel close to each of you," "I don't make friends so easily, this was quite something," "I am a reserved and shy person. Noticing how we open up right off the bat, it makes it easy with all," "we already showed up for each other," "there is a commitment to each other."

Celebrations and milestones

To strengthen the commitment to the group, it is helpful to regularly invite the group members to celebrate their journey. What benefits have they received from the group? What are milestones that they remember for each member and for the group? These are powerful questions to ask.

Regular celebrations about the group's milestones reinforce cohesion. Milestones include: once each member has received at least one instance of group coaching, anniversaries of the start of group, New Year, start of the Summer, etc. Such celebrations are an opportunity to reflect on the group's learnings, strengths, and needs.

Forming the group outside of the group coaching sessions

Interestingly, research has shown that creating the conditions for relationship building between members before the start of the group sessions does not impact the development of cohesion.

However, once the group coaching intervention has started, it seems that informal group meetings are beneficial. Members of some of my groups organize theatre outings, host dinners at their homes, or meet at the restaurant or a rooftop bar. Members do not expect me to attend. When I choose to join them, I show up as a guest and not as a group coach.

Reflective questions about Chapter 3

- The chapter presents an ideal picture of curation. Most of the time, the context in which we operate forces us to make trade-offs. From your perspective, which aspects of curation are the most important and why?
- How does cohesion in group coaching compare to the strength of the coach-client relationship in dyadic coaching?
- Thinking about your strengths and development areas as a coach or a group coach, what aspects of psychological safety do you feel the most equipped to foster?
- What other techniques would you add to foster cohesion and psychological safety in a group of women leaders?

Bibliography

Brandmo, C., Aas, M., Colbjørnsen, T., & Olsen, R. (2021). Group coaching that promotes self-efficacy and role clarity among school leaders. *Scandinavian Journal of Educational Research, 65*(2), 195–211.

Brown, S. W., & Grant, A. M. (2010). From GROW to GROUP: Theoretical issues and a practical model for group coaching in organisations. *Coaching: An International Journal of Theory, Research and Practice, 3*(1), 30–45.

Carroll, M., & Shaw, E. (2013). *Ethical maturity in the helping professions: Making difficult life and work decisions*. Jessica Kingsley Publishers.

Clark, T. R. (2020). *The 4 stages of psychological safety: Defining the path to inclusion and innovation*. Berrett-Koehler Publishers.

Edmondson, A. C., & Lei, Z. (2014). Psychological safety: The history, renaissance, and future of an interpersonal construct. *Annu. Rev. Organ. Psychol. Organ. Behav., 1*(1), 23–43.

Feghali, A. (2022). Executive peer advisory groups: who they are? What are their benefits? Why do members join and stay? *Dissertations, 930*. https://digital.sandiego.edu/dissertations/930

Flückiger, B., Aas, M., Nicolaidou, M., Johnson, G., & Lovett, S. (2017). The potential of group coaching for leadership learning. *Professional Development in Education, 43*(4), 612–629.

Forsyth, D. R. (2021). Recent advances in the study of group cohesion. *Group Dynamics: Theory, Research, and Practice, 25*(3), 213.

Fumoto, E. (2016). Developing a group coaching model to cultivate creative confidence. *International Journal of Evidence Based Coaching & Mentoring*.

Knight, C. (2017). The mutual aid model of group supervision. *The Clinical Supervisor, 36*(2), 259–281.

Mansfield, E., Jalal, N., Sanderson, R., Shetty, G., Hylton, A., & D'Silva, C. (2024). Digital storytelling online: A case report exploring virtual design, implementation opportunities and challenges. *Research Involvement and Engagement, 10*, 43.

Parker, P. (2020). *The art of gathering: How we meet and why it matters*. Penguin.

Van Dyke, P. R. (2014). Virtual group coaching: A curriculum for coaches and educators. *Journal of Psychological Issues in Organizational Culture, 5*(2), 72–86.

Yalom, I. D., & Leszcz, M. (2020). *The theory and practice of group psychotherapy*. Basic Books.

Chapter 4

The High Performing Coaching Group

Key points of Chapter 4

✓ One of the most important roles of the group coach is to foster creativity in the group. This is achieved primarily through the activation of group dynamics, adequate support to the presenter and to the group members who are coaching.

✓ An effective group coach models and uses eclectic approaches to creative thinking, to deploy creativity techniques that involve multiple senses, and activate not just to rationality and logic but also emotions and bodily sensations.

✓ Supporting the application of learnings is also an important role of the coach, recognizing that most of this happens in between-sessions and in conjunction with other interventions.

✓ As mentioned in Chapter 1, the group coach offers an evidenced-based structure for the group coaching process as well as evidence-based methods to support it. In my practice I use Action Learning, supported mostly by conversational methods such as active listening, solution-focused questions, appreciative inquiry, narrative coaching, and visual-based storytelling.

Purpose of Chapter 4

"Making your unknown known is the important thing." I love this quote by Georgia O'Keefe which resonates for me because the main purpose of group coaching is to support the generation of new leadership development insights for the group members. The generation of new insights is the result of a creativity process, a new mental combination of information that one

DOI: 10.4324/9781003465195-5

already possesses with new information that one has received. The recombination is triggered by serendipitous connexions in the brain. In group coaching, participants receive multiple sources of new information, not only when they are receiving support but also when they provide support. The group enhances the reflective process of each member. It fosters the emergence of new ideas that build on one another.

In this chapter, I start with a review of techniques that foster creative reflection for the presenter and for the group. In the second section of the chapter, I discuss the interventions that the coach can use to deepen creative reflection. In the third section, I consider techniques that facilitate the transformation of these reflexions into applicable learnings. Finally, I discuss the implementation of evidence-based approaches and models to group coaching.

Creative reflection in group coaching

The role of the group coach is to support the generation of new insights for each individual member by activating the group, the presenter, and the individual group members who coach her.

Managing expectations

I do not believe that each member must receive coaching in a particular session. Indeed, from a client-centred perspective, no-one may predict how long a particular coaching round is going to take. As a result, I make it very clear to group members that we will most likely not coach everyone in a session, and that I will keep track of presenters to ensure that each members gets a turn regularly.

However, I promise my group members that I will manage the scope and the time of each round carefully, in collaboration with the group, so that the presenter and each group member feels a sense of completion. Indeed, each coaching round is a container, it must be opened and closed. The following questions help the group members feel a sense of completion:

- "Where are you now?"
- "What has been achieved at this stage?"
- "What else do you need to feel complete?"
- "What are the next steps?"

Women leaders are high achievers and results oriented. They set high standards for themselves and show a tendency for perfectionism. They may expect that a group coaching round ends with a major insight. But there are times when the presenter does not share the ha-ha moment that everyone is hoping for. The coach can help group members' focus on the process and not just on the result, and appreciate the benefits of the journey itself, such as feeling supported, healed, or affirmed.

Activating the group

The management of group dynamics is the responsibility of the group coach, who can lean on members whose personality traits are most conducive to promote psychological safety and creativity in the group.

Kets de Vries (2014) identified two levels of dynamics at play in group coaching. The first level is the group dynamics that support the coaching of the presenter. For example, the group coach might invite the group members who coach the presenter to offer more open-ended questions. Additionally, the group coach might manage the share of voice of each group member to maximize the diversity of shared perspectives.

The second level is what he calls "the cloud," which he defines as the resonance of the presenting issue to each group member. Resonance can be directly linked to a recognition or realization that the group member shares the same issue as the presenter. It can also refer to emotions related to the issue that comes back to the surface as the discussion unfolds (guilt, shame, jealousy, etc.). In that role, the group coach pays attention to the quality of interactions between group members. If some behaviors are undermining rather than supporting learning, the group coach will bring them to the surface and interrogate the group.

Specific attention must be brought to cultural differences in creative thinking, which should be acknowledged and viewed as a learning opportunity for the group. For instance, some cultures promote divergent thinking and some prefer appreciative inquiry. In group supervision, the group leader's multiculturality has been associated with greater satisfaction for group members and has contributed to the development of their own intercultural skills.

Even with careful curation, there will be instances when one or a few members have little to contribute to the presenting topic. The group coach role is to invite these members to think about the learning opportunity for them, and to share it with the group. This will put other members at ease and is likely to promote hope (that the member's needs have been addressed, and that their needs will be addressed should they find themselves in a similar situation). When a member holds a very different viewpoint from others, the coach should emphasize that this member's opinion, while unique in this group, might be held somewhere else in their environment, and that it is therefore useful to hear it. This will promote safety and encourage the sharing of different perspectives.

Supporting presenters

In some instances, the expertise of the group coach may be needed to help generate presenting issues or to support with the presentation of issues.

Generating issues

It is not uncommon for women leaders to arrive unprepared to a group coaching session. In this case, I offer a reflective slide and some time (no more than five to ten minutes) for silent individual reflection. The reflective slides offer an opportunity to scan the last few weeks, in various life compartments. The supportive questions are very basic and general to give as much space as possible to the member:

- What's working well?
- What's not working so well?
- What would you like to learn more about?
- How can the group support you today?

Presenting an issue

It can be useful for the coach to add one or two questions to the reflective slide mentioned above, which will help the presenter focus the group on what really matters.

- What is going on? What is your desired outcome? What options are you considering?
- What most frustrates you about the situation? What most excites you?
- Who are the key stakeholders involved in the situation with you? What relational shifts have you tried? What has worked and not worked?
- What emotional shifts have you tried for yourself? What has worked and not worked?
- What else feels important to share?
- What support would you most like to receive from the group today to help you think through your challenge/opportunity?
- What is the briefest description you could give to the group to help them support you?

Asking the right question to the group

The group members who coach the presenter must know what is expected of them. I always request that the presentation of the issue ends with a clear statement of what is needed from the group. In the following example,

Carnation does not want open-ended questions. Instead, she is requesting stories.

> **Carnation** would like to spend more time networking internally and externally so that she can increase her influence in her organization. However, she never makes it a priority, always finding excuses that there is too much to do.
>
> **Carnation's question to the group**
>
> How do you get yourself motivated to network more?

Collective group coaching

There are situations when no group member has anything to present. This can't be predicted, which means that a group coach should rely on pre-prepared thought-provoking questions about a common topic that is likely to resonate for the group. Common topics will have typically surfaced during mutual introductions, or they can come from the group coach's own research. The questions should activate story telling so that vicarious learning can be maximized.

Changing attitudes to work, cybersecurity, artificial intelligence, a more volatile economic environment, political polarization and geopolitical crises, climate change, are common environmental challenges experienced by leaders. I have noticed that women in my group appreciate, from time to time, the opportunity to discuss how these environmental changes impact them as a leader, especially when a crisis happens.

> **A member responds to the prompt: what is the opportunity of the Covid crisis**
>
> **Aster** is a mother of young children who owns a training business. When the Covid pandemic started, she viewed the crisis as an opportunity to launch a digital offering. However, she was not sure of her ability to scale up.
>
> **Aster's question to the group**
>
> What questions should I be asking myself to decide if this is the right move or not?

Interventions from the group

- What has been your appetite for financial risk in the past?
- What is your personal comfort level balancing your family needs with your business needs?
- What is missing for you from your current business that you are hoping to get by adding a digital offering?
- What decisions could you make now that could later be reversed?
- What are your core values telling you?
- What if this business was outsourced?

Aster's key takeaways

- I want to explore what it is that I am truly looking for in my career. Must I fulfil this need by adding a digital offering?
- I love the rule of regret-minimizing and will apply it as I decide my next step
- I feel liberated and see a way forward.

While they recognize the impact of systemic biases, women leaders in my groups have been more interested to discuss adaptive individual strategies than to plan for social change. The most important topics revolve around six core themes:

- increasing their motivation (meaning, alignment, authenticity, celebrations, values, joy, leveraging strengths, crafting a personal purpose)
- managing their energy (fighting burnout, identifying depleting and energizing activities, self-care, delegation, boundary-setting, letting go of perfectionism, guilt management, conflict management)
- increasing their visibility and influence (self-confidence, brand-building, voice, risk taking, fighting bias, limiting beliefs)
- framing hardships positively (acceptance, dealing with the aftermath of a precarious promotion, self-compassion, self-efficacy, opportunities, job transition)
- increasing opportunities to connect (relationship building, strategic networking, inclusive practices, mentoring, communities/shared experiences)
- managing career phases (portfolio careers, career shifts, Board membership)

Table 4.1 below gives examples of common topics. At the end of the proposed questions, I encourage the group members to add their own with a prompt such as: "What questions do you have for the group?"

Table 4.1 Examples of collective group coaching topics for senior women leaders in my practice

Topic	Sample reflective questions
Addressing geopolitical events	• How do you anticipate which geopolitical topics are likely to affect your organization and your team? • What criteria do you use to decide whether to speak up or to stay silent? • What approaches do you use to foster constructive dialogue? • How do you take care of yourself and others in your organization during these times? • From your experience: What are best practices and worst practices when addressing geopolitics?
Asking for help	• Complete the sentence: as year 20 starts, the most important matter I need help with is… • What values, emotions, thoughts, or images are triggered in you when you contemplate asking for help about this matter? • Reflecting on past experiences asking for help (good and bad), what best practices would you like to share?
Psychological safety in teams	• As a team member, what have been your best and worst experience of psychological safety as a team member? • As a team leader, what best practices have you developed to foster psychological safety within your team? • To what extent is psychological safety embedded in your organization's culture? • What barriers are you experiencing in promoting more psychological safety in your organization?
Making more time to network	• What are your top three reasons to want to network more? Where are you looking to expand your network? • In what ways is your networking intent connected to your leadership vision or purpose? • How open and diverse is your current network? To what extent does it give you access to broader, more diverse networks? • What are your strengths as developer and nurturer of high-quality relationships? How can these be leveraged as a networker?

(Continued)

Table 4.1 (Continued)

Topic	Sample reflective questions
Dealing with difficult personalities	• What personality traits are difficult for you to deal with? • What impact do difficult personalities have on you? • How do you take care of yourself when dealing with difficult personalities? • What have you learned about your strengths when successfully managing difficult personalities? • What have you learned about your development needs when being unsuccessful? • What best practices would you like to share?
Responding to constant solicitations	• Who solicits you? What for? • What emotions are triggered each time you receive another solicitation? • How are the constant solicitations impacting you? What are you saying no to when you accept solicitations? • What is your approach to prioritizing solicitations and setting boundaries? • What makes setting and/or sticking to your boundaries hard? • What is working to protect your boundaries?
Transition and personal change	• What important transition is on the horizon? • What is it asking you to leave behind? • What is it allowing you to keep? • What is it offering you to start? • What can you prepare for? • How can you inject joy into the journey?

Activating the contribution of group members

Even if they have experience with managerial coaching or mentoring, women leaders may need help reconnecting with their coaching skills. Their first go-to approach is sometimes to give advice. In the final section of the chapter, I will discuss coaching models that can help them formalize more effective coaching behaviors. In this section, I focus on two skills that are important to remind the group members: asking open-ended questions and giving situational behavioral feedback.

Open-ended questions

There are many lists of open-ended questions that the group coach may want to share with the group. But the group coach needs to think carefully. Women leaders who participate in group coaching do not expect to learn coaching techniques. Instead, they expect to leverage the power of the group to get insights. As a result, my approach is to let them lean on their own managerial coaching experience. My preference is to emphasize best practices. When I notice the positive impact of an open-ended question, I typically ask the presenter about her experience. This helps everyone else in the group internalize the power of a great open-ended question. Here are some of the best practices that I have noticed in my groups:

- less is more: one deep question will have more impact that multiple shallower questions
- keep your curiosity in check
- veiled advice ("have you tried X") does not invite dialogue with the presenter. Questions such as: "I have tried X. What do you think?" or "What are the pros and cons of X from your perspective?", or "I have tried X. What else have you tried?"
- one question at a time: don't stack up questions
- give the presenter time to think and fully answer the previous question before asking the next question

Giving feedback

In my groups we use a situational behavioral feedback protocol. The model unfolds in three phases. In the first phase the feedback giver relates a behavioral observation to a specific situation. It sounds like "when we talked about X, you looked angry," In the second phase, the feedback giver describes how the behaviour impacted her and others. It sounds like: "once I noticed that you looked angry, I really did not want to upset you. So, I decided to abort the discussion." In the third phase, the feedback giver asks the following question: "What is your perspective on what happened?".

The main advantage of situational behavioral feedback is that it depersonalizes the feedback, which becomes a description of a situational behavior followed by a consequence. It is particularly effective in cultures in which the experience of shame is undesirable. Generally, it contributes to building psychological safety in the group.

Here is how the protocol might unfold in a group coaching context:

Situation: Zinna has been in a conflict with her boss for several months now (Situation: an on-going conflict).

Behavior: Zinna keeps bringing this same issue to the group coaching session. She does not implement the ideas that were discussed previously (Behavior: bring the issue over and over to the group coaching sessions without reporting any progress).

Impact: Sage shares that she feels the stuck-ness in Zinna's situation and that she feels helpless and frustrated. After a pause, she asks how the rest of the group feels about this. One by one other group members share similar feelings (Impact: everyone feels stuck).

Takeaways: Sage asks Zinna: What are you learning from this? Zinna thinks for a moment. Then she reflects that she has heard the same reaction from her colleagues at work. She thanks the group for the feedback and says that she needs to think about this more. At the end of the group coaching session, the group coach asks for key takeaways. When it's her turn, Zinna shares her realization that she needs to change the narrative and must tell her story in a different way if she wants to get help and be more resourceful (Takeaways: changing the narrative).

There is plenty of evidence that a group is one of the most powerful spaces to process feedback. In fact, the psychodynamic group coaching model uses the sharing of 360 feedback results as a starting point. Presenters take turn sharing their emotional reactions to the report, good or bad. Using either a Balint or Action Learning format, the group members share their own perspective about the presenter's report and ask questions of the presenter.

Summarizing

To help the group move a group coaching process along, the group coach can summarize the key phases of the group dialogue so far. The group coach can also add a summary of previous conversations that the group might have had on the same type of issue, either with the same presenter or with a different presenter. From there, the coach may invite the group to explore patterns and to offer more questions to the presenter.

The eclecticism of the group coach

In previous research, I asked clients of dyadic coaching which coaching behaviours generated the most creativity for them. What surfaced was the importance of eclecticism. Clients like to benefit from great questions, of course, but also from receiving a reaction (this is how your situation lands on me), some useful information (informing rather than advising), or from a relevant experience of the coach.

In group coaching, I invite members to use the full range of these verbal behaviors, above and beyond open-ended questions. Once I sense that the group is running out of questions, I prompt them by asking:

- What else might be relevant to the presenter, any experience, advice you have received in the past?
- How has the conversation impacted you so far? What emotions are you experiencing?
- What question has the presenter not asked to the group that you were expecting?

Elevation

Sometimes there is an opportunity to elevate a presenter's issue that is described as a tactical challenge to a leadership challenge. I recall a situation when a member needed help asking for a raise. I acknowledged that this was an opportunity for one-on-one support after the session. I then asked the presenter how she felt about the situation. When she mentioned frustration and helplessness, I asked the group how it resonated with them. The conversation evolved into supporting the participant with her negotiation skills.

Polarity management

The group coach has a role to play to enhance the quality of the group coaching process by managing the polarity support vs. challenge. When the group is overly challenging to the presenter, I offer supportive questions. Reciprocally, when the group is too supportive to the presenter, I add a more challenging question.

Appealing to different senses

You may be familiar with the concept of learning styles, that distinguish auditory, visual, and kinaesthetic learning. Research has shown that these styles are both personality and situation dependent. We generally think of coaching, let alone of group coaching, as an auditory activity. Yet, there is a sizeable body of knowledge that demonstrate its effectiveness can be enhanced if combined with visual and kinaesthetic activities, as shown in Table 4.2 below.

Table 4.2 Verbal, visual, and kinaesthetic representations of a presenting issue

	Verbal	Visual	Kinaesthetic
Individual issue	The presenter verbalizes the story	The presenter describes an image or a metaphor	The presenter describes and moves objects that have been placed on a table
Collective issue	Each group member reflects individually and verbalize their perspective	Each group member describes an image or a metaphor that represents their perspective	

Group coaching with visual metaphors

Research indicates that visual metaphors convey complex information more effectively, by providing a more efficient neural path towards cognitive empathy and factual understanding. They provoke serendipitous new connections in the brain, which is a precursor of creativity. They showcase the commonalities in the members' experience and deepen the experience of universality and normalization. More recently, the case has been made that visual metaphors may increase the motivation to achieve one's goal.

There are multiple ways visual metaphors can be used in group coaching. For example, the group coach might suggest that each group member introduce themselves with an image, or that a presenter proposes an image to describe her presenting issue. To illustrate the approach, I will describe the Head, Heart, and Gut protocol. In this method, group members are asked to draw a representation of themselves based on the three dimensions of Head, Heart, and Gut. Taking turns, each group member describes their drawing to the other group members. The other members react or ask questions. The Head, Heart and Gut protocol is a deep multimodal introductory approach to explore group members' personal identity, leadership strengths, career aspirations, etc. I do not recommend using it online.

Table 4.3 Presentation of the Head, Heart, and Gut protocol instructions to the group

Dimension	Components	What to draw
HEAD	Cognition	Expertise
	Pattern recognition	Learning style
	Reasoning	Talents
	Abstraction	Education
	Analysis	Task orientation
	Synthesis	Fact orientation
	Semantic processing	
	Language	
HEART	Emotional processing	Family
	Values	Friends
	Relational affect	Relationships
		Core values
		People orientation
GUT	Core identity	Creative expression
	Safety	Likes and dislikes
	Boundaries	Use of intuition
	Aversions	Originality
	Impulse for action	
	Gutsy courage	
	Willpower	

Group coaching using kinaesthetic learning

Kinaesthetic approaches are useful when exploring a presenting issue from a systemic perspective. In this section I describe the use of the constellation technique, an approach pioneered in family therapy. In group coaching, this systemic approach consists of using small objects that each represent a stakeholder (or a group of stakeholders) involved in your challenge or opportunity. It is best to use objects that are directional. This approach is best used face to face.

Caspia has just been hired as the CEO of a start-up owned by a larger company to launch a digital offering line. The COO of the larger company is the Board Chair of the start-up. The other Board Members are also leading other businesses of the larger company, some of which may be cannibalized by the new digital offering. The COO is ambivalent about the potential of the digital product offering. Caspia as the support of the CEO, who is the COO's boss.

Caspia asks the group to help reflect on navigating her relationships with the Board Members to activate their support for the new digital offering. There is a selection of random office objects available, which Caspia can

Figure 4.1 The representation of a presenter's system using the constellation approach.

choose from. On the table she places the lighter to represent herself and the candy box to represent the new business. The jar lid represents her ideal relationship with the Board. The CEO is the marker, and the COO is the highlighter. Business leaders are the paper clips.

When they ask questions, group members are invited to move the objects on the table. For example:

- moving the lighter behind the highlighter: What can you compliment the COO on? How can you make her feel that you respect her business insights?
- moving the marker and some of the paper clips facing towards her behind the paper clips facing away. Who is most likely to influence the business leaders who feel threatened by the new digital offering?

At the end of the conversation, Caspia is invited to reflect on the results of the new design. This leads her to plan an influence project and prioritize the most important conversations that need to take place.

Using an emotion-based approach

I like to describe emotions as warning signals on your personal dashboard. Becoming aware of an emotion and its intensity invites the group members to surface the critical nuances of a presenting issue. There are a few questions that I might offer to the group or to the presenter if I sense that the room is emotionally charged:

- As you share the issue, what are you noticing about the emotional impact on you?
- What might be the emotional impact on the other stakeholders in this issue?
- How is this issue impacting others in the group?
- To what extent are these emotions helping or hindering our work together?

Using an embodied perspective

The use of physicality in coaching has been often prescribed but poorly researched. My usage of it is minimal: I am looking forward to more evidence-based models. When members describe the physical sensations that they experience and the body language that they observe when a presenting issue is discussed, I have noticed that it helps illuminate aspects that were previously hidden to the presenter. As a result, I encourage it by asking questions similar to those that I use for the exploration of emotions. For instance, I might ask the group members: "Did you notice any shift in the presenter's body language when she presented her issue?", "What did you notice in your body when you listened to the presenting issue, when we discussed the presenting issue?". I might also ask the presenter what they have noticed in themselves and in others when they were presenting or discussing the issue.

A few years ago, a member of one of my online groups was a trained yoga instructor. She accepted to lead us in short series of desk yoga movements at the start of each session. Many members and I noticed a marked difference on our own energy and concentration levels.

A related aspect of embodied coaching is outdoor coaching. While there is still little empirical evidence of the benefits of coaching outdoors, benefits of conducting other helping interventions outside, such as psychotherapy or education, have been surfaced. They include improved cognitive functioning, concentration, attention, mood, and stress recovery. The outdoors generates a sense of connection, even when they are seen from a window. In my practice, I have noticed a sharp contrast in concentration and energy between group coaching sessions conducted in windowless rooms and group coaching sessions conducted in rooms with windows giving on to large fields of vision, especially of nature. I have also noticed a burst of energy whenever we were able to engage in group coaching in a confidential outdoor space.

I have successfully incorporated walking dyadic coaching in my practice. I would welcome suggestions to experiment with group coaching while moving in nature.

Applied learning in group coaching

Setting expectations

Not all members are in a place where they can share a fully formed goal at the end of a session. A group coach should not pressure them to do so: it's not the main objective of group coaching. However, because many members have been formatted to think of coaching (including group coaching) as a goal setting vehicle, there is often an underlying expectation that a goal is a natural ending to a group coaching session. Some members might feel guilty if this is not the case. In addition to sharing a key takeaway, I offer some questions to ponder as members leave the session. For example: What intention are you leaving with? What progress are you looking forward to sharing at our next meeting?

Verbalizing key takeaways

In my groups, presenters are asked for their key takeaways at the end of their coaching round. In addition, each member of the group is asked for at least one takeaway at the end of the session. This verbalization helps participants experience a sense of completeness and consolidate the learnings.

Two days after the session, I send the group one paragraph with my own key takeaways from the session, in the hope that it will further reinforce these learnings.

Asking other members for help in between group sessions

As I mentioned, in the contracting phase with the group, I recommend to members that they should minimize tactical advice during the group coaching sessions and take it offline. As a result, members in my group often contact each other from the starting place of advice-giving. It often evolves into a peer coaching relationship, which produces an effective combination with group coaching.

Experimenting and reporting back to the group

New learnings will be reinforced and refined by engaging in experiments between group sessions. At the end of the group session, when applicable, I encourage members to share if they are committed to testing an alternative perspective, to experimenting with a new behavior and to sharing their learnings during the next call.

In Table 4.4 below, members first share a significant professional achievement that was achieved building on the support of the group. Then, they ask the group for help to further leverage this achievement.

Table 4.4 Experimenting and reporting back to the group

Achievement reported back to the group	Next steps shared with the group
Thank you to the two members who gave me feedback on my employment contract	I need a sounding board to prepare my first Town Hall announcing my ideas to capture low-hanging-fruit
Thanks to the group, I feel more organized and grounded in the process of my job transition	I need a sounding board to explore how I can bring more fun into my life without feeling guilty
The group helped me realize that I need to come from a place of vision as I implement a major restructuring of my division	How can I balance hope and realism in my approach?
The group helped me regain my self-confidence and gave me the push I needed to launch my online business	I notice some remaining anxiety over delegating childcare duties and business administrative duties. How can I unlock myself?

Sharing meta-learnings

Organizational learning theory proposes that meta-learning, the process of reflecting about how and when learning occurs (or does not occur) increases the understanding of members about the conditions of successful group coaching. As a result, I regularly invite my groups to reflect on the quality of their learning and collaboratively design new processes that can improve the group's functioning.

Structure and models of group coaching

This section is best understood if you read or re-read Chapter 1, pages 21–22, where I provide an overview of the evidenced-based approaches to group coaching.

In my practice I use the Action Learning group structure. As a reminder, it consists of five phases.

1   the presenter explains the issue and asks a question of the group
2   the group asks a few clarifying questions
3   the group and the presenter discuss the issue
4   the presenter shares key takeaways
5   the group reviews the experience

In group coaching, it is expected that in the third phase group members deploy coaching behaviors to help the presenter with their issue. I am not a fan of using structured coaching models to guide the deployment of coaching behaviours. Rather, I like to lean on the managerial coaching skills and knowledge that exist in the group. As I have mentioned before I do not insist that group members only ask open-ended questions. On the contrary, I invite a mix of sharing experiences, reactions, relevant information, followed by an open-ended question to the presenter such as: How does this resonate for you?

As I mentioned above, group members will spontaneously offer to support the presenter through advice giving. Once it is out of the way, they can tune back into their listening skills. Typically, they will deeply listen to the issue so that they can help them identify the important underlying needs (zooming in), give them tailored advice (mentoring), and ask them for their takeaways (zooming out).

Typically, women leaders will offer excellent questions to help the presenter assess the situation:

• What do you want to happen?
• What would that look like?
• What is the real issue?

- What have you tried?
- How is that working or not working?
- What are you afraid of?

Additionally, they are proficient asking questions to generate next steps and accountability:

- What can you control/influence/accept?
- What do you plan to do next? When?
- What will you begin doing differently?
- How will you know you are successful?
- How will you stay committed?

As a group coach, we can build on these strengths. In addition, we can invite them to expand their repertoire of powerful questions to foster new insights for the presenter. Some groups need more help than others. In that case, I rely on evidence-based coaching models that are quick and easy to understand.

Practicing listening skills

This approach to group coaching creates awareness that, above and beyond the presenting issue, there are other dimensions that can be listened to.

In this modified Balint group process, once the presenter has stated her issue, I ask the group to stay away from problem solving and to focus on what they have noticed while they were listening. Instead, I suggest that members focus on the following:

- What facts have been shared?
- What assumptions have been made?
- What emotions have you noticed in the presenter, in yourself, in the room while the issue was shared?
- What values surfaced that are important to the presenter as she was sharing the issue?

After the group has discussed each question, I ask the presenter to share their key takeaways.

> **Celosia's** co-owner has announced his intention to retire soon. He has taken his foot off the pedal while keeping the same compensation, which impacts the business. Celosia's objective is to buy back his shares and to become the sole owner of the business. Every time she tries to bring up the topic, he has a way to avoid the conversation.

Celosia is concerned that he might not really want to retire, that there is something else going on she cannot identify. She believes that now is the time for the big conversation, but she feels unprepared emotionally and tactically for the negotiation.

Celosia's question to the group

How can I prepare myself?

Group's responses

- Facts: 20 years as a co-founder. Business partner says he wants to retire soon. He produces less. He has kept the same compensation. There is a financial impact on the business. He avoids the topic. He does not know Celosia's objective.
- Assumptions: he has taken his foot off the pedal. He has not really decided what he wants to do.
- Emotions: Celosia is ambitious, determined, focused, confused, frustrated, impatient, unprepared, resentful. Group members feel triggered, angry, impatient, curious, hopeful, determined.
- Values: fairness, hard work, result-orientation, transparency, honesty, trust.

Celosia's takeaways

- I feel out a brain fog
- I must define clear steps
- I put too much pressure on myself for this conversation: it's just a beginning

Solution focused

In this situation, once the presenter has described her issue, I give a few minutes for everyone to scan the solution-focused questions, once section at a time. Then, I invite group members to ask their preferred questions and the presenter to respond. At the end, I ask the presenter which additional questions she would like to answer.

Section 1: Preferred future

- What does an ideal outcome look like?
- Suppose you have been successful, what are you doing?
- What are you noticing is different?
- Who else is noticing? What are they noticing?
- How will you know it is in place/achieved? What will that look like?
- What are the progress clues?
- What else would you like to ask (or be asked)?

Section 2: What's already working

- What is already in place?
- What impact have you had?
- What have you already tried/achieved/discussed?
- How have you handled this previously?
- What is working well?
- What is not working?
- What is getting in the way?
- What is missing?
- What have you considered might work?
- What else would you like to ask or be asked?

Section 3: Next steps

- What else can you try?
- How else might you explore/consider/approach this?
- What will help you move one step forward?
- Who else can support you with this?
- What are the next step options?
- What are you willing to do?
- What most excites you?
- What else would you like to ask or be asked?

Marguerite is the owner of a successful niche design company. When she pitches new business against larger firms, she feels less accomplished than her competitors. When she networks with other women leaders who work for larger companies, she feels like a fraud.

Marguerite's question to the group

I would like guidance and insights on how to overcome my imposter syndrome

Group's interventions

- What would you feel like if the size of a company was not important for others?
- What do other women who own small businesses think or feel?
- Thinking of your current client base, what do think made them choose you over larger businesses?
- What are the positives of owning a small business?
- What is behind your concern of owning a smaller business?
- What are you proud of concerning your small business?
- When networking with others, what do you bring to the conversations?

Marguerite's key takeaways

- I am inspired to capture pride stories I have about my business
- I will challenge myself to be a speaker on a panel in my professional association chapter
- I am excited to report my progress back to the group

Appreciative inquiry

Appreciative inquiry is a powerful generator of insight once the group members know each other well. As one of my group members expressed: "remembering the positives and learning from successes is so much more energizing and unlocks me."

The process is to ask group members to share which strengths they have experienced from the presenter that can be applicable to their presenting challenge.

- What are her most significant strengths?
- In what ways have these strengths manifested to you?
- Which strengths are applicable to her presenting issue?

A group uses appreciative inquiry to help each member reflect on their challenge

- Mink's challenge is to grow talent in her business to make it even more attractive to a prospective buyer. Applicable strengths surfaced by the group include: encourages, clarifies, mentors, courage, perseverance, sees different sides of a problem, drives accountability.
- Godetia wants to have a conversation with her boss to convince him that his proposed reorganization has more drawbacks than advantages. The strengths experienced by the group that are applicable to her challenge are: reasonable, approachable, passion to improve, listening, pragmatic, efficient, intellectually curious.
- Daffodil's objective is to develop a long-term plan to exit her current business and start the next stage of her professional life. Strengths that were surfaced include: strategic, option generator, activator, fun, creative, listener, relationship-building, reflective.
- Dahlia is planning a change of ownership structure for her business. Strengths that she was encouraged to activate are: tenacity, hard-working, risk-taker, creative thinking, purpose, confidence.

Narrative coaching

In the previous chapter, we have seen how story telling builds cohesion in the group. In this section we examine how story telling supports the generation of new insights for both the narrator and the listener.

Leveraging decades of research in psychotherapy, Drake has developed a narrative coaching theory that states that story telling helps clients develop new narratives and unlock themselves. This process occurs when the coach becomes curious with the storyteller about how the narrator situates themself in their stories, what frames they use to describe their context, and whether such views might be self-limiting. In group coaching, multiple listeners will enhance the power of this investigation.

From the listener's perspective, studies in multiple social science disciplines have shown that exposure to relevant narratives will bring changes to personal beliefs and attitudes, by engaging both cognition and affect.

Not all women leaders have had the opportunity to hone their story telling skills. The group coach has an opportunity to assess the quality of each participant's story telling skills in the forming stages of the group. For members who are less competent, the group coach can encourage them to visualize the impact that they want their story to have on the group. For example: "What do you want each of us to think, feel, and do after hearing your story?"

Dianthus would like to spend more time networking internally and externally so that she can increase her influence in her organization. However, she never makes it a priority, always finding excuses that there is too much to do.

Dianthus' question to the group

How do you get yourself motivated to network more?

Stories shared by the group

- I have a role model, a friend of mine who is not afraid to sell herself. She pushes me to experiment with new behaviors
- I start with my most pressing influence projects. The more connected it is to my work need, the more motivated I am to start it
- I don't like networking either. I am part of a women networking group where interactions are organized for me
- I reach out to former colleagues I have enjoyed working with. They never let me down
- I have found that asking my colleagues for help strengthen the relationships

Dianthus' key takeaways

- I feel I am not alone with this problem
- I appreciate the tips to trick myself into networking
- I will experiment with them and report back

Reflective questions about Chapter 4

- What is your perspective about the respective roles of the group coach and group members to foster creativity and insight generation in group coaching?
- When supporting a group or an individual that is struggling with creative thinking, what are you go-to methods?
- After reading this chapter, which insight-generation methods would you like to try and why?
- What is your experience using visual or kinaesthetic approaches to group work?
- What have been the responses of the participants?
- How applicable are your preferred dyadic coaching approaches to group coaching?

Bibliography

Berta, W., Cranley, L., Dearing, J. W., Dogherty, E. J., Squires, J. E., & Estabrooks, C. A. (2015). Why (we think) facilitation works: Insights from organizational learning theory. *Implementation Science, 10*(1), 1–13.

Burn, A. S., & Passmore, J. (2022). Outdoor coaching: The role of Attention Restoration Theory as a framework for explaining the experience and benefit of ecopsychology coaching. *International Coaching Psychology Review, 17*(1), 21–36.

Davis, C. H., Gaudiano, B. A., McHugh, L., & Levin, M. E. (2021). Integrating storytelling into the theory and practice of contextual behavioral science. *Journal of Contextual Behavioral Science, 20*, 155–162.

Drake, D. B. (2017). Working with narratives in coaching. *The SAGE handbook of coaching*. London, UK: SAGE, 291–309.

Jackson, P. (2017). Physicality in coaching: Developing an embodied perspective. The SAGE handbook of coaching, 256–271.

Kets de Vries, M. F. (2014). The group coaching conundrum. *International Journal of Evidence Based Coaching and Mentoring, 12*(1), 79–91.

Prywes, Y. & Mah, E. (2019). Seeing Polaris: A call to integrate visual images into coaching action plans. *Philosophy of Coaching: An International Journal, 4*(1), 34–56.

Scholtens, S., Kiltz, L., Boer, H., Konkolÿ Thege, B., & Fleer, J. (2023). Conceptualisation of the systemic organisational constellation method and a procedure for its application in coaching. *Coaching: An International Journal of Theory, Research and Practice*, 1–15.

Seto, L., & Geithner, T. (2018). Metaphor magic in coaching and coaching supervision. *International Journal of Evidence Based Coaching and Mentoring, 16*(2), 99–111.

Soosalu, G., Henwood, S., & Deo, A. (2019). Head, heart, and gut in decision making: Development of a multiple brain preference questionnaire. *Sage Open, 9*(1), 2158244019837439.

Chapter 5

Managing Disruptions and Changes in a Group of Women Leaders

Purpose of Chapter 5

In this section I examine the role of the group coach as a detective. Like Hercule Poirot in *Murder on the Orient Express*, the group coach asks "What other explanation can there be? [...] That is what I ask myself [...] is what I never cease to ask myself." Indeed, the journey of the group is not linear. As we mentioned in Chapter 1, the group is a complex adaptive system.

DOI: 10.4324/9781003465195-6

Disruptions and changes occur internally and externally to the group. The group coach should feel equipped to address breakdowns such as ruptures of cohesion, disruptive member behaviors, problems of communication between members of the group and disruptive group behaviors.

Managing ruptures of cohesion

As I mentioned previously, there are two dimensions of cohesion in a group: horizontal (member to member or member to group), or vertical (member to group coach). In this section, I suggest ways to address breakdowns in each dimension.

Managing ruptures of horizontal cohesion

Even a high functioning group may encounter ruptures of horizontal cohesion. Indeed, every member may experience, at some point during the group coaching journey, transformational learning moments. These moments may or may not come from the group coaching process. They may have been generated by events that the member has experienced between two group coaching sessions, including personal or professional losses or setbacks. Depending on the personality of the group member, the realization that individual change is necessary to overcome a challenge will be destabilizing and stressful. The capacity of a group member to respond to stress constructively varies based on the intensity of the stress and the time needed to rebound.

When a group member is temporarily destabilized or stressed, the group coach must work to repair any impact this situation might have on the psychological safety experienced by all members in the group.

Sunflower's voice is resentful. She reports being furious and helpless, once again, with her boss. This time, he has suddenly decided to change bonus rules to the detriment of the staff in the division she manages. Sunflower disagrees with the rationale of the change and the method of communication. She has assessed that there is no room for negotiation with her boss.

Sunflower's question to the group

How can I best manage myself to deliver the bad news to my division in a constructive way?

Group's contribution

The group is torn and two lines of questioning surface. One part of the group believes that Sunflower needs to explore her fit with her boss and the organizations' culture (Leave!). Another part of the group believes that it's part of a leader's role to deliver news that they don't agree with (Shape up!).

Sunflower's reaction

Both lines of questioning are challenging for Sunflower. She is fearful about contemplating the idea that she might be misaligned with the company's culture. And she feels guilty of coming across as a victim when sharing her challenge. She thanks the group and responds, rather curtly: thank you, I'll think about this.

The group is unsettled. One of the members who had advocated "Leave" asks how she can support Sunflower. There is a long silence after her question.

How would you address the rupture of horizontal cohesion surfaced in this example? In my research about effective coaching behaviors from the client perspective, I surfaced transparency as a major skill to maintain trust between the coach and the client. Reflecting on, and sometimes refining rules of engagement helps restore psychological safety. Reminding everyone that the group is not always the best source of wisdom or information takes the pressure off the members and may help restore self-confidence and mutual trust. In addition, the group coach might notice that some questions may sound like disguised advice or opinion, and invite the member to reflect on the impact that her intervention had on the presenter.

Managing ruptures of vertical cohesion

Research in group dynamics indicates that when a rupture of trust occurs between the group leader and one member during a single session, it will have a negative impact on this member's group coaching outcome on that day, regardless of their average level of vertical trust experienced so far. As a result, a vertical rupture should be taken very seriously and investigated by the group coach.

When you are openly challenged by a group member during a session, acknowledge the challenge. Remind the group that you welcome feedback.

Invite the member to schedule a one-on-one conversation for this purpose. Get back into the group coaching process as quickly as you can. Do not get other members involved in the conflict. This will damage your credibility and negatively impact the cohesion of the group. Always remember that you are working for the group and not for the challenging member. During the follow-on, one-on-one conversation with the member who challenged you, ask for situational behavioral feedback. In other words, ask the member to explain what happened, what behavior you displayed and what was the impact on them. Invite the member to continue giving you feedback as needed and remind her it is always best done one-on-one.

Low satisfaction scores received after a session are a sign of rupture of trust.

- If you know who gave you the low score, connect one on one with the member and ask them how they can feel better supported. Often, you will discover that the member has doubt about her fit with the group, which you will need to address.
- If individualized feedback is not available, reflect on the topic of the low score (for instance: poor time management). Be transparent with your group at the next coaching session and tell them what you have been thinking about. Invite the group to recontract with you so you can better address their needs going forward.
- In some situations, you might get a low general satisfaction score without any comment. Again, be transparent with the group and walk them through a general feedback exercise, using a very simple indirect feedback approach. For instance, what's working for you/what's not working for you.

If you are sensing that something is not working well, without being able to identify it, remind members that they are welcome to share feedback offline. Ask for feedback at the end of a session from time to time. At the risk of repeating myself, two culturally sensitive questions to ask remain: "What worked well for you today in the session?" and "What did not work so well?".

Disruptive individual behaviors

Disruptive individual behaviors compromise the cohesion of the group and/or the generation of new insights for each member. Most of these behaviors can be avoided through good curation and strong shared ground rules.

Minimizing the occurrence of disruptive individual behaviors

It is very important that the coach adopts a partnering approach with the group members instead of an expertise approach when discussing disruptive individual behaviors. Women leaders are not students waiting for you to teach them group dynamics concepts. Arguably they are experts themselves. They lead inclusively and do not let such behaviors compromise the performance of their own teams. When they experience these disruptive individual behaviors in the executive teams that they belong to, they are aware of their negative impact and attempt to mitigate them.

As a result, a collaborative discussion about the rules of engagement in a group, is indispensable if you want to build vertical cohesion. In my groups we talk about conducive individual behaviors, including consistent attendance, punctuality, balanced share of voice between members, positive conflict management techniques, inclusive language, confidentiality, etc.

We also agree that each group member is responsible for their own behaviors. We encourage each member and the group coach to name and to challenge other members' behaviors when they are disruptive to the group, by providing situational behavioral feedback in real time.

Minimizing the impact of disruptive individual behaviors

Disruptive individual behaviors that most impact cohesion include lack of punctuality, monopolising discussion time, engaging in power struggles with other group members or with the group coach, interpersonal conflict, active or passive aggression, superficial or non-participation, use of disrespectful or inappropriate language, sarcasm, violent or explicit content, disclosure of unlawful activities. Table 5.1 below suggested possible approaches to minimizing the impact of these disruptive individual behaviors in a group.

Psychodynamics in group coaching

While a group coach is not expected to be trained as a psychotherapist, a working knowledge of psychodynamics is useful to surface the root causes of some irrational behaviors during the session. The group coach must be able to detect whether resistance, transference or countertransference may interfere with the performance of the group.

Resistance

When one or several group member(s) often refuses to abide by or to enforce the agreed upon rules of engagement, this could be a sign of resistance. Here are possibilities to explore, in Table 5.2 below.

When the coach notices these behaviors and helps the group explore resistance from a place of compassion, it allows members to reflect on themselves at a broader level. Where else are these resistances playing out in their lives? How they can support others at work or at home who are experiencing resistance?

Table 5.1 Proposed approaches to challenging individual behaviors

Disruptive behavior	Proposed approach
Member does not attend consistently, frequently arrives late, leaves early, or goes in and out of meetings	Call the member individually, ask them for news. Name the behavior and explore its impact on the group. Ask the member whether they can commit to the group at this time or if they need to take a leave of absence.
Member is overly competitive or self-centered	Interrupt and summarize the member's contribution. Gently remind everyone that we get as much from helping others than from receiving help. Invite group members to offer their perspective. If issue persists, call the member after the meeting to give them personalized feedback.
Member shares unsolicited opinions or advice	Ask the recipient how this impacts them. Remind everyone that sharing stories is more powerful than giving advice, and of the power of open-ended questions.
Member is expressing strong emotions	Take the time to acknowledge the emotion. Hold the boundaries according to the ground rules. Capture learnings from the member and from the group.
Member is dominating	Interrupt and summarize. Remind the ground rules. Invite other members to offer their perspectives. If the issue persists, call the member after the meeting to give them individualized feedback.
Member is overly quiet	Send agendas in advance. Carve out five-minute preparation time using a reflective slide. Call them out. Build on their contribution. Ask them to share their experience in the moment.
Member challenges your competence	Acknowledge. Complete the task. Ask the group whether they would like to carve out time at the end of the meeting to give you some feedback.

Table 5.2 Examples of members' resistance in group coaching

Behavioral symptom	Nature of resistance
Gives unsolicited advice	Resists to feeling helpless
Multitasks during conversations	Resists to feeling overwhelmed
Criticizes the process	Resists to feeling inadequate

Transference

This phenomenon happens when a group member transfers to the group a relational feeling that they have experienced in the past, elsewhere in their life. It is often manifested in sudden emotions or irrational reactions. Here is an example. A few years ago, I received feedback from a group member that my level of executive presence was insufficient. I asked her for more context. Instead of responding to my prompt, she shared that she had received the same feedback when she took her first leadership position in the United States. She was asked to take accent reduction classes to remedy the problem. She did so, but it did not help as much as she would have liked to. She continues to wonder whether her accent impacts her credibility. It so happens that I speak with a noticeable French accent. As a result, I asked her how she felt about my accent in my role as a group coach. She reflected and said that in fact my accent did not matter at all. I asked her if there was anything else she wanted to give me feedback on. She said no, and we ended the conversation. From then on, she successfully bonded with the group and stayed on for the next two years.

Countertransference

Countertransference refers to the response of the coach to transference. When the group member project their own emotions on the coach, it is possible that the coach will also experience strong reactions and emotions.

Here is the rest of the story. After the conversation with this member, I started to experience strong anxiety before each group session with women leaders. With my supervisor we explored the situation from two perspectives. Subjectively, I shared that I had lost a client bid, 20 years ago, because they had said my accent that was too strong. Suddenly I was projected back years ago when I was full of self-doubt growing my practice. Now that I had surfaced the issue, I felt complete. However, later on, I reflected that my own anxiety gave me access to the experience of a woman leader's anxiety, starting her own coaching journey, and also the anxious experience of other group members. This led me to collect more information about the members' state of mind, and to adjust the speed at which we moved along the group coaching process as needed.

When a member is not a good fit with the group

How to do you detect a member who is not a good fit with the group? When this is a curation issue, trust that the member will let you know that they need another group to thrive. It's more complex when the member is unaware that their behavior jeopardizes the health of the group. Examples include:

- Complainers/victims or manipulators who blame you and/or the group for issues that they are responsible for.
- Members with unacknowledged dysfunctional group attitudes who struggle with self-awareness. Behaviors include constant interruptions, dominance, and a desire to take over your role, jumping in to give advice, discounting other's issues, oversharing about their own complex medical, psychological, or spiritual issues, oversharing personal views about trending topics, inappropriate expression of political or religious views.

After a few sessions, if you notice that a member has a blind spot that might impact their own learning or that of the group, gently probe the member, during the session, by sharing patterns that you have observed across several sessions. Once you have shared, pause, and ask: "how does this resonate for you?" and then ask the group the same question. This will not only help the member in the moment but will also encourage group members to emulate your approach. For example, I had a quiet member in one of my groups who frequently needed prompting to share what usually turned out to be a very powerful contribution. Once, she brought up her issue managing a difficult relationship with a peer. I stated what I had noticed in the group setting. Other members volunteered that they had noted the same thing. The quiet member offered to experiment with being more assertive in the group and to reflect on how she could apply her learnings to her relationship with her peer.

The two values that I call forth in these difficult situations are courage and compassion. I call the member, give them situational behavioral feedback, and ask them for their perspective from a place of openness and curiosity. I then offer to brainstorm with them what other spaces might be a better fit to their needs. To prepare for and follow-up on these calls, I usually seek support from the company sponsoring the group coaching initiative, from my own supervisor and from my peer supervisory group.

Whatever the outcome of these difficult conversations, I have made my own the Four Agreements of Don Miguel Ruiz:

- "Stay impeccable with your word"
- "Don't take it personally"
- "Don't make assumptions"
- "Always do your best"

If I assess that I have fulfilled these commitments to myself, I feel complete.

When a group member leaves

The departure of a group member may create uncertainty in the group. When I start a group, I remind everyone that members may leave a group for multiple reasons, so that the process can be normalized. The departure of a group member is an opportunity for the group coach to learn. I am always grateful if a member takes the time to share their experience of the journey, but I never push them to disclose their reasons for leaving if they don't want to. I am open to the possibility that a departing member may want to say goodbye during their final group sessions. It's an opportunity to appreciate the departing member while strengthening the cohesion of the group. After the group member is gone, there might be a need to discuss the impact this is having on the group, and I create a safe space for it.

Problems of communication

Communication theory has conceptualized the most common problems that can surface during a group conversation. Most of these issues arise in group coaching as well. In this section I provide a description of these problems and suggestions to address them.

Judgement

I mentioned earlier in the group the importance of modelling situational behavioral feedback techniques within the group. As a result, I remind group members to give any feedback by starting with "I-statement" rather than a "You-statement."

Veronica is hard on herself. She just shared a story mentioning that even though she achieved an important milestone with her team, she is not sure this will be enough to be promoted. Notice the difference between reacting: "You should feel proud of your achievements with this team" and reacting: "I felt so proud of you when you share your achievements with this team." Hearing the first sentence, Veronica might feel judged and guilty of being so low in self-confidence. Hearing the second sentence, Veronica is likely to feel energized, and can tap into this energy to become more resourceful.

Advocacy

When a group member is particularly persistent in pushing their point of view, the group coach can invite the group to acknowledge the behavior and become curious about it. Where does the members' insistence come from? Is it coming up at work? At home? Where is the learning opportunity for the member?

Anger

Anger is not an unproductive emotion; it can be the start of a call for action. When a member expresses anger, take the time to listen and allow the anger to run its course. Quickly summarize the thought expressed and acknowledge the emotion. Invite other members to share how it lands on them. If the member needs recovery time, apply the rules discussed for a member in distress, as mentioned below.

Distress

If the presenter experiences distress, do not make assumptions. Trust them to tell you if they want to continue or not. If another member is affected by what was said, protect the presenter's slot and invite the other member to take care of themselves until the group coaching round is complete. If the distress continues, ask the member how they can be helped.

Oversharing might also be a sign of distress. Help the member focus their attention by gently interrupting her. Then, ask if there is something common to all they said that is worrying them the most.

Resignation

Some presenters will resist other's inputs with responses such as "I've already tried," "Yes, but," "I am not sure this can work" utterances. The use of paradoxical injunction will help. For example, we could agree that the presenting situation is hopeless. Such statement opens to the door to a conversation about acceptance.

Ruptures of flow

Communication theory has identified six typical behaviors that impede the flow of the discussion.

Let's take the fictional example of Tulip. She is the only woman in the executive team and can't find her voice as the new CMO. Her peers constantly challenge her as if they had more expertise than her. Her CEO is conflict adverse and does not support her when this happens. Here is a sample of unhelpful reactions from other group members:

- Tangential reply: "Maybe you should hire a voice coach?"
- Switching: "Men always have this way to shut down women's voices"
- Status disqualification: "In my experience, everyone thinks they are a better CMO than the CMO"
- Redundant question: "Why is this a problem?"
- Mystification: "This has nothing to do with you. You are new to the role, give it some time"
- Evasion: "I think everything has already been said"

In this scenario, the group coach can ask Tulip how each of the questions landed on her, so that members realize that there is a gap between their intention and their impact. This gives a chance to the group coach to unpack the behavior and its impact.

Microaggressions

While there is little research on microaggression between members in group coaching, it might become an issue when groups are diverse. Members whose social identity is underrepresented are likely to take longer to feel psychologically safe in the group. If they experience a microaggression that is not processed, the cohesion of the group will suffer. At the same time, it is important to recognize that addressing microaggression is likely generate fear in most members of dominant groups, which will also adversely impact cohesion. In addition, addressing microaggressions too directly will violate social norms in some countries.

To encourage group members to surface microaggressions when they happen, there are two approaches:

- Having a conversation about microaggressions as part of the rules of engagement. This is not my preferred method because it might induce anxiety and fear, and these emotions will not be acknowledged because the psychological safety of the group is not strong enough yet.
- Waiting until the group has a strong cohesion and organize a reflective segment on the experience of diversity in the group. Questions such as: what is your experience belonging to our group where members have diverse social identities? What social identities are present in this group? How is this different from your experience at work, or in your families? How has your own social identity shaped you as a leader? What would you like to pay attention to, as group? How can we support each other? This is my favourite approach.

Difficult group situations

Sometimes it's the group dynamics that requires the coach's attention. Once a group dysfunction has been identified, I engage in single-loop, double-loop, and triple-loop learning with the group. Let's illustrate the process for a group who meets online, later in the day, and tends to be apathetic.

In single-loop learning, the coach invites the group to reflect on the impact of group apathy on group effectiveness. For example, when we are apathetic, we don't contribute that much, and we learn less from each other.

In double-loop learning, the coach supports the group to brainstorm on solutions. For instance, members might reflect on ways to increase the energy of the group members when they enter the space. They might decide to start each session with some stretching exercises.

In triple-loop learning, the coach would suggest that the group designs a protocol to surface and process any new group dysfunction that might arise in the future.

Common group dysfunctions

In Table 5.3 below, I have compiled some common group challenges and a proposed approach to address them.

Table 5.3 Challenging group dynamics and how to address them

Challenge	Proposed approach
Members are anxious, overly competitive, disinclined to share, show poor listening	These attitudes adversely impact the psychological safety of the group. To rebuild it, spend more time building trust in the group by offering exercises that help them share more about themselves. Overuse appreciative inquiry techniques. Ask members to share their experience and take-aways at the end of the session.
The group holds unconscious or unspoken conflicts	Conflicts impact the cohesion of the group. To restore it, call out inconsistencies and gaps in the functioning of the group. Encourage members to share their perspective and feeling. Facilitate a group feedback exercise. Recontract as a group.
The group is apathetic and overly reliant on you for substance	Apathy impacts vicarious learning and the generation of insights. To address this, always have a short prompt ready to elicit the sharing of presenting challenges or opportunities. Invite the group to revisit common topics. Invite the group to prepare open ended questions together, so that they can reflect on these topics in future meetings.
An external crisis impacts several members of the group	An external crisis that affects some group members may impact the safety of all. To restore it, hold the space to allow those members to share how the event impacts them. Invite the group to reflect on adjacent leadership topics (example: how to address the crisis with your team, on behalf of the organization, etc.)
A group dwindles down	Once a group drops under five participants, vicarious learning drops, and the power of the group to provide insights diminishes. As a coach, you will start playing a more active role in the coaching of each member. Ask members how they feel about this. Offer to merge with another group as needed.

(Continued)

Table 5.3 (Continued)

Challenge	Proposed approach
Two smaller groups are merging	Psychological safety and cohesion need to be rebuilt. When you have not coached one of the merging groups, hold a one-on-one or a group on-boarding interview (if feasible) to capture the hopes and expectation of the small group and to share your approach. When the merged group meets for the first time, you will need to repeat, at an accelerated speed, the group forming activities mentioned in Chapter 3. I also recommend that you alternate presenters from one group and from the other.
A group is ending	This typically creates anxiety and guilt in group members. Encourage the group to acknowledge what has been accomplished, and each individual member to share what they are looking forward to for the rest of their journey.

Emergence of a conflict of interest or loyalty

In Chapter 3, I recommended to actively weed out potential conflicts of interest or loyalty when curating a group. Unfortunately, changes in the composition of the group or changes in the life or career situation of a group member or another stakeholder may generate or bring to the surface unforeseen conflicts. As we will discuss in the next chapter, the best practice is to bring these issues to supervision or to a trusted peer. In certain situations, you might need help from a lawyer.

A breach of confidentiality

A few years ago, the coaching service provider who contracted me hired a close friend of a member of one of my groups. The group member, unbeknownst to me, disclosed confidential information that was shared during our group coaching session to offer support to her close friend. The close friend reached out to me to express her disagreement about the substance of what was shared (and interestingly, not about the breach of confidentiality). After consulting with my supervisor, I requested a three-part conversation to repair the trust and re-establish ground rules.

Digital group coaching

Since the Covid pandemic, the delivery of group coaching digitally by video has become ubiquitous. In this section, I share my best practices when using video group coaching with women leaders. They include:

- Provide an agenda in advance and remind the group of the link.
- Request video on, for everyone.
- Be even more inclusive in your facilitation. In addition to be sensitive to different learning styles, personalities, and identities, you should also pay particular attention to the environment from which each participant logs into the call. Certain exercises (dance or yoga movement, raising their voice, etc.) may not be possible for everyone. Some participants like to comment or ask questions on chat while the conversation is going on. Do not assume that all participants are able to read them. Speak these out as needed.
- Stay away from the spotlight. Beware of talking too much and avoid long slide decks. Not only is this too coach-centric, but it also impacts cohesion and collaboration by preventing participants from seeing each other. My rule of thumb: no more than one slide, on which participants quickly reflect individually in preparation for a collective discussion.
- Spend more time watching the body language of participants. Does anyone look distracted or disengaged, has someone stopped showing their face to the camera?
- Be more direct and assertive in your facilitation: use your voice more than body language
- Be even more structured (clear beginning – middle – ending)
- Provide a brief linkage between group activities so that participants can explicitly move from one to the next.
- Be very strict with time. Most participants will jump right into the next meeting and will not appreciate missing the end of the group call.
- As a rule, keep technology as simple as possible during the video call. A shared digital whiteboard, or a link to complete a survey on the fly, or even the sharing of images, may not be easily accessible to everyone during the time they are on the call. Do not assume that everyone is on a device where they can easily use their screen interactively. And do not assume that everyone is familiar accessing and using interactive tools. While the percentage of digital natives is growing in the women leader ranks, we are not at 100%.
- If everyone is comfortable with ad-on software, research shows that this will enhance creativity by appealing to participants' various senses and learning styles. In that case, I recommend that you seek the help of a technical co-host to handle digital operations.

- Recording and transcribing may go against data privacy laws in some countries. Check applicable laws. Be particularly careful when members connect to the call from different countries.
- Remember that some organizations block access to certain communications platforms from a company-issued device. Some countries may also block access to certain video call platforms for geopolitical reasons.

Reflective questions about Chapter 5

- What stories, emotions or bodily sensations come to mind when you think about the various dysfunctions evoked in this chapter?
- What other kind of dysfunctions have you experienced when working with groups?
- When addressing a dysfunction, how do you manage the polarity between personal boundaries and flexibility?
- What is your experience of digital group work vs. face-to-face group work? Would you add anything to the list provided on page 131 of the chapter?

Bibliography

Gerndt, U. (2014). Frederic Laloux Reinventing organizations. *Presentation slides*. Internet [Accessed June 30, 2017]. Available from: http://www.reinventing organizations.com/uploads/2/1/9/8/21988088/140305_laloux_reinventing_ organizations.pdf

Miles, J. R., Anders, C., Kivlighan III, D. M., & Belcher Platt, A. A. (2021). Cultural ruptures: Addressing microaggressions in group therapy. *Group Dynamics: Theory, Research, and Practice*, 25(1), 74.

Ruiz, D. M., & Mills, J. (2011). *The Four Agreements (Illustrated Edition): A practical guide to personal freedom* (Four-color Illustrated Ed.). Hay House, Inc.

Tasca, G. A. (2021). Twenty-five years of group dynamics: Theory, research, and practice: Introduction to the special issue. *Group Dynamics: Theory, Research, and Practice*, 25(3), 205.

Thornton, C. (2010). *Group and team coaching: The essential guide*. Routledge.

Visser, M. (2007). System dynamics and group facilitation: Contributions from communication theory. *System Dynamics Review*, 23(4), 453–463.

Chapter 6

The Future of Group Coaching
Human Capacity and Artificial Intelligence in Service of Women Leaders

Key points of Chapter 6

✓ More research is needed about the societal impact of group coaching for women leaders. How can the group coach navigate societal and multicultural evolutions?

✓ There is a lack of evidence about which capacities are the most important to develop for a group coach of women leaders, including personal qualities, ethical maturity, and deliberate practice.

✓ There is no theorization nor competency model for group coaches, which prevents its professionalization and adaptation to specific populations such as women leaders. What can be inferred from research in its root disciplines?

✓ It seems reckless to develop safe AI systems for the group coach until we have a well-researched capacity model for the group coach, and a collaborative system in place between researchers, practitioners, and developers.

Purpose of Chapter 6

As Henri Bergson said: "To exist is to change, to change is to mature, to mature is to go on creating oneself endlessly." The purpose of this chapter is to address two fundamental emerging developments in group coaching and propose future topics for research. The design of a capacity model for the group coach and the emergence of artificial intelligence in group coaching. From my perspective, it will be very difficult to adequately design AI systems if we don't have a solid conversation about what capacities, competencies, and skills are needed for a group coach who serves women leaders.

DOI: 10.4324/9781003465195-7

Toward a capacity model for the group coach of women leaders

Building a capacity model, as presented in Figure 6.1 below, requires operating at four hierarchized levels.

The first, foundation level is social and multicultural: what is the function of group coaching women leaders in relation to social challenges and global issues?

The second level is intrapersonal: who is the ideal group coach for women leaders? Which qualities need to be cultivated?

The third level is theoretical: what is the theoretical stance of the group coach and what evidence supports recommended approaches, tools, and techniques?

The fourth level is technical: what knowledge and skills are needed to deploy these approaches, tools, and techniques?

The purpose of group coaching for women leaders

The purpose of group coaching is to support the achievement of individual leadership development goals. Arguably, as I have shown in Chapter 2, my current group members prefer to use group coaching to navigate their present environment rather than to call for its radical change.

At the same time, many women leaders are on the frontline of social and multicultural transformations in their organization. They are often expected to drive Diversity, Equity, and Inclusion initiatives. Their collaborative and empathic leadership style, and their own experience of exclusion, makes them more aware than men that organizational structures that rely on the "perfect worker" model are not sustainable. As described in Chapter 1, the

Figure 6.1 A proposed hierarchy of research needs for coaching groups of women leaders.

"perfect worker" operates under an outdated patriarchal model. They are family provider, who for a duration of 40 to 50 years, dedicate all their energy to work while other family members take care of all other life responsibilities.

Women leaders make use of their group coaching sessions to reflect on how to motivate a diverse workforce who is committed to the organizational objectives as long as they do not exclude them from engaging in other life compartments. As a result, they are involved in the collective conversation on social change. In fact, social constructivist theorists believe that that the group coach may need to act like a social movement activist. In such capacity, the group coach would hold a space to help members reflect on their values and causes, and on how to act on them, by building alliances inside and outside of the group.

From a pragmatic perspective, since the social topics will come up, the group coach must be prepared to support sessions focused on these. This has implication for their professional development. Indeed, they must develop a deep awareness of their own beliefs and attitudes, notice her own biases and feelings, practice cultural humility and perspective taking and be compassionate to themselves and to others.

I believe that the first step on the group coach development journey is to become conscious of your own personal experience and how it has shaped you as a practitioner. Have you lived in different countries? Which dimensions of your social identity belong to a dominant group, which dimensions belong to an underrepresented group? What are other group coaching practitioners saying? How are they leveraging their unique experiences?

The next step is to have a sound appreciation of other cultures. Having lived and worked in four different countries myself, I have noticed social identity markers did not hold the same weights. Class is important in the UK, race is fundamental in the US, race and religion are conflated in Malaysia and in addition there is a divide between local and expatriate leaders. In France, my native country, one's educational background is an important social marker. Overt discussions about some types of intersectionality are not appropriate in certain countries and may even be illegal. While there is no way anyone can become a multicultural expert, the group coach must be aware of which cultural dimensions are important to take into consideration in their group. The cultural blindness of the group coach might do more harm than good and might set back efforts to promote women's representation in certain countries.

The self of the group coach

The self of the group coach and their capacity to serve women leaders deserve more research. In Figure 6.2 below, I represent the role that the

Figure 6.2 Difference between the role of the group coach, facilitator, and educator.

group coach can play, and how differently balanced it is from the role of the facilitator or educator. The role of the group coach is best summarised in this quote by Mazzolini & Maddison (2003): "Sage on stage, guide on the side, ghost in the wings." The group coach is rarely on stage, and mostly to remind group members of the rules of engagement. The rest of the time, the coach is a guide on the side, if the group needs help leverage its dynamics, or a ghost in the wings, when the group coach simply holds the space while group members thrive.

I like to compare the group coach to the founding member of a leaderless team. In this model, members of the team self-manage, and there is no hierarchy. The group is viewed as a living entity. Another metaphor that comes to mind is that of the conductor of a big band in jazz. Notice how the conductor gives the initial impulsion to the big band, then get to the side of the stage, and comes back, from time to time, to acknowledge or indicate a change of cadence or theme.

To embody and balance the three roles, the group coach must let go of two extremes: being a solar lead, at the centre of the group, and being a laisser-faire lead, on the side of the group. If a coaching group were a movie, the group coach would neither be the star of the show, nor just a spectator. Navigating these polarities, knowing when to jump in and out, checking the group's pulse, are fundamental capacities of the group coach.

The group coach must be deeply self-aware, spot their own limitations, navigate them in the moment and reflect on them afterwards to find out if they must and can be addressed. Indeed, unacknowledged resistances of the coach can impede the team dynamics. Here are a few examples. A group coach who is in the grip of her own cultural norms might fail to listen from a perspective that will be helpful to move the group's conversation forward. A group coach life narrative may block their listening or hold them back. A coach might experience countertransference (which we have explored in the previous chapter). All these issues, if unaddressed, will impact the safety, courage, and compassion of the group coach.

Should the group coach be a woman?

In dyadic coaching, research shows that the gender of the coach has no significant impact on the outcome of coaching. In group coaching, there is no research on the matter. However, we have explored in Chapter 1 the advantages and disadvantages of mix-gender leadership development interventions. Based on this research, I infer that a group coach who identifies as a woman is likely to have an advantage over a man when building vertical cohesion. Yet, I have surfaced before that it is horizontal cohesion, not vertical cohesion which has the most impact on a high performing group. Clearly, more research is needed.

Personal qualities of the group coach

Who you are is how you will coach your group. Are there different ways of being when coaching a group of women leaders vs. a mixed-gender group? Here are a few considerations that might guide future researchers:

- Authenticity: this is especially important for women leaders, who often struggle to develop authentically in their careers, due to the patriarchal norms that continue to exist. The more you can model your own authenticity and celebrate it in others, the better.
- Humility: as a group coach you are not the primary helper, and not the centre of attention, except when setting or reminding ground rules for the purpose of attending to the group dynamics. Remember that you are holding the space for a group of women leaders who are most likely to be very skilled in team building.
- Improvisation: Kets de Vries has compared the dyadic coaching process with jazz improvisation. This is particularly relevant in group coaching, an even more complex adaptive system, where it is impossible to predict what is going to happen next. A group coach should be highly tolerant of complexity, ambiguity, and contradiction.
- Letting go: there are moments of synergy when you need to trust the potential of the group to take full control of the coaching space. I recall an unsettling but deeply instructive moment in my practice. In the middle of an online group coaching session, my internet connection shut down for 15 minutes. When I finally came back online, the group had progressed naturally, and the presenter was just beginning to share their key takeaways!
- Authority when needed: the group coach is the keeper of the rules and is the ultimate decision maker when it comes to the management of the group dynamics. Use authentic and appropriate advocacy methods to take back control when needed.

- Energy management: as in any group work, there is bound to be some personalities or topics who energize us and some who drain us. The group coach needs to recognize this for themselves and for each member of the group. The group coach is here to maintain the collective energy of the group and recognize when a pause (for meta-learning purposes) and a shift need to take place to restore it.
- Awareness of psychological safety and other hidden processes: it is the group coach's responsibility to notice and surface potential ruptures of group dynamics
- Presence: the group coach should be aware of their own internal response to the group's actions and use these as one as supplementary data at their disposal to manage the group coaching space. Negative emotions should be used as alarms, as invitations to rethink and improved the group coaching process, rather than being repressed.

Ethical maturity in group coaching

Ethical maturity stands on two foundations: the ethics of means and the ethics of results.

Deontology is the ethics of means. There is no research indicating that ethical guidelines should be different whether the group is women-only or is mixed-gender and perhaps this should be explored.

While there is no research on ethics in group coaching, the team coaching ethical charters produced by accrediting bodies, enriched with other sources, may serve as a starting point:

- coach the group as a single entity
- avoid conflicts of interest and minimize conflicts of loyalty between you and the group members, and within the group membership
- hold the boundaries between group coaching and group psychotherapy
- demonstrate that you have learned evidenced-based group coaching competencies
- explicitly and appropriately move in and out of the three roles you play during a session (facilitator, coach, educator)
- help to establish and remind group rules, especially confidentiality rules

Considering the ethics of results, some may hold a utilitarian perspective, selecting what produces the greatest utility for the group. Other may prefer a virtue approach, basing their decisions on a set of values.

Regardless of your chosen stance, I like to ask myself the following questions, which I have adapted from the work of Michael Carroll and Elisabeth Shaw:

- Would I recommend this course of action to someone else?
- How comfortable would I feel if others were doing what I am about to decide?
- Could I defend my position in front of a committee?
- What would the wise people in my life say?
- If there was media coverage, would it make me proud?
- Could I explain my decision with honour to my loved ones?

Reflective practice

Reflective practice allows the group coach to reflect on their skills in relation to their capacities.

To support reflexivity, theorists of adult development describe several states of thinking that one can engage with, from the simplest to the most complex. While several models exist in the literature, they commonly identify stages that build on each other. The basic stage fulfils one's personal, existential needs. The intermediate stages include the need to belong, which invites compliance; the need to be recognized, which leads to expertise; the need to achieve, which leads to result-orientation; and the need to redefine, which leads to creativity. At the highest levels, humans express the need to transform and achieve wisdom.

A group coach who is focused on their professional development needs to be conscious about the levels from which they need to operate in relation to that of the group members.

When the group coach fails to effectively display a particular group coaching skill timely, it could be because they do not have enough knowledge, enough experience, or enough theoretical understanding of the skill. This can be addressed with more mentoring and more training.

However, skills are just the tip of the iceberg. What if the lack of skill were a symptom of insufficient reflexivity? Reflexivity is not just fed by your own internal feedback systems, it is also informed by external feedback which you can collect from the group, and from other stakeholders such as the commissioner, the coaching service provider, your supervisor, or a peer.

Do not neglect any of these sources. Research has identified a "Rashomon effect" in the perception of coaching behaviors and of their impact, depending on the observer. In other words, each stakeholder observes a similar event through different lenses, leading to widely different accounts of what happened.

Once you have collected multisource feedback, there are several techniques that you can use to make sense of it. You might process the feedback using a "Johari window" a method often used in multi-rater assessments, which helps you detect potential blind spots or unacknowledged strengths.

The awareness of gaps arises by comparing your self-assessment of strengths and development needs with what was observed by others.

When you need to change a behavior, the "Discounting model" offers a multi-level reflective framework, which can be used on your own or with the support of your supervisor.

- select a group coaching behavior that you want to change
- focus on the situations in which the behavior was at play
- reflect on the impact it has on clients and other stakeholders
- explore tools and techniques to change your approach
- assess if you have the necessary skill set to deploy them
- if needed, plan how to acquire the skill set
- identify and work to overcome any self-imposed barriers to get started with your supervisor

Underlying theories and evidence

The next level on Figure 6.1 is the capability of the coach to decide when and to what extent a specific model of group coaching should be deployed. This decision is based on the underlying theories of group coaching and on the evidence that has been collected on existing approaches, tools, and techniques. In this section I simply want to reiterate how important it is that every practitioner chooses and articulates their ontological, epistemological, and theoretical preferences, and understands how it informs their practice.

Personally, I am a pragmatist practitioner. Because I believe that truth is expressed when a group of people agree to identify and solve a problem together, I partner with the group on the process of group coaching as well as on the content of group coaching. I favor group-centred theories and methods. I follow research closely, especially mixed-methods and action-learning research, because I believe in a strong collaboration between researchers, practitioners, and clients.

If I were a positivist practitioner, I would consider myself as an expert. As a result, I would take the lead and drive the process because I believe that I know better. I would be closely focusing on the latest research on leadership. I would ensure the group members are aware of the most updated effective leadership competencies. In terms of theories and models of group coaching, I would favor those that have been evidenced-based, if possible, through quantitative research methods.

If I were a post-modernist practitioner, I would invite the group members to draw from their individual experiences to drive the group process and would adopt a laisser-faire approach. I would promote self-compassion, self-care, and engagement for social change. I would closely follow qualitative research and encourage the group to experiment with emergent approaches.

Accreditation and certification for group coaches

At the final level (Figure 6.1), the group coach needs a skillset. As I have mentioned previously, the main accrediting bodies have yet to publish a competency model for the purpose of certifying group coaches. As a result, experienced facilitators, team coaches, dyadic executive coaches, as well as group supervisors, whether certified or not, operate as group coaches and learn along the way.

A few schools of group coaching are accredited to deliver courses that will count towards certification as a dyadic coach for their students.

If group coaching is to follow the path of dyadic and team coaching, we can expect that sponsors will require a certification from their group coaches in the years to come.

To anchor the certification process, job analysis research is needed, such as what was conducted by the International Coach Federation for dyadic coaching and for team coaching. Table 6.1 below summarizes what the academic and practitioner's literature has surfaced as specific group coaching competencies.

Table 6.1 Proposed competency model for the group coach

Strategizing and decision making

- Optimize the curation of the group
- Co-create group agreements, boundaries and working methods
- Manage the timing of the session. Ensure that there is an explicit beginning, middle and end. Ensure the group stays on track.
- Remind group agreements and lead the redesign of group agreements as needed
- Evoke awareness, encourage participants to pause and reflect, to notice assumptions, to question powerfully
- Foster mutual aid
- Teach simple and effective group coaching techniques
- Model effective feedback (situation, behavior, and impact)
- Model active listening: summaries, paraphrases, follow-on questions
- Establish collective progress and accountability as a group
- Facilitate reflective learning at the individual and at the group level
- Model effective communication: calm, confident, succinct, clear, explicit, direct, inclusive, check for understanding
- Encourage the group to own the dialogue: ask probing questions, redirect questions to the group, recall earlier discussion outcomes, give positive reinforcement, offer a new perspective if nothing else works

(Continued)

Table 6.1 (Continued)

Individual and group development

- Cultivate trust between group members
- Cultivate psychological safety within the group: encourage the sharing of ideas and feelings, stay neutral and non-judgmental (on substantive matters), ensure that each member has an opportunity to share
- Model empathy, compassion, and wisdom
- Model vulnerability: when you don't know, tap into the wisdom of the group
- Meet ethical guidelines
- Hold the space and structure of the group coaching session
- Understand, notice, call out and manage group dynamics and dysfunctions
- Notice and manage inter-personal conflicts and micro-aggressions
- Bring to light individual behaviors that impact the collective energy, engagement, and focus of the group
- Educate the group in how to work more effectively by encouraging meta-learning

---

Artificial intelligence and group coaching

Artificial intelligence (AI) refers to machines performing human cognitive functions, without human guidance. Due the nature of a group coaching as a complex adaptive system, I assume a future in which AI is fully powered by machine learning instead of being rule-based. I introduce the distinction between narrow AI, focused on a narrow range of activities that assist the group coach, and general AI, which is supposed to perform all the activities of the group coach.

As I finish this book in March 2024, no general AI can reproduce the capacity and skillset of a mature group coach. Machine learning systems do not know that they are affecting their environment. They possess no self-reflective capacity, no ability to recognize themselves in relation to others. While AI will offer non-judgmental and neutral advice on the surface, it is not clear how machine-learning recycles and reinforces current human biases. This may be particularly relevant for the group coaching of women leaders. Indeed, machine learning is based on algorithms trained on data sets. Currently, there is no control over what these data sets are. They may incorporate the individual biases of those who select the data sets, they may reflect existing prejudices about women leadership. Arguably, most programmers are men, and few have deep experience about group coaching, let alone of the specific needs of women leaders.

The problem is that the machine learning process is completely dependent on the data sets. AI cannot allow what they cannot imagine and cannot understand that they might be mistaken. As a result, AI is not yet able to assess whether a decision will lock us into a situation where we are unable to pursue a different objective under a different context. Without ways to circumvent these limitations, general AI remains unsafe and unethical for the purpose of group coaching women leaders.

However, I am not as definitive about narrow AI. In Table 6.1 above, I have proposed to organize the competencies of the group coach using two categories: strategy and decision making, on the one hand, and individual and group development, on the other hand. Let's explore the case for additional research and experimentation with narrow AI in relation to these two categories of competencies.

Strategy and decision making

When reviewing the strategic and decision-making competencies of the group coach, there are promising developments in narrow AI. However, a major caveat is bias in the construction of the systems. It remains unclear whether the data used to produce the recommendations is reflective of the needs of women leaders.

Curation support

- analyzing participant's readiness for group coaching based on their response to an enrollment questionnaire
- curation of a group and matching with a group coach based on their response to a questionnaire

Logistical tasks

- scheduling the group coaching sessions
- on-boarding the group coaching participants with an interactive presentation video

One-on-one coaching for group members between group sessions

A conversational agent (also called a chatbot) can coach individual group members between group sessions. As I complete this book, six are already available on the market, but are not tailored to specific populations. Based on data analysis (recording of progress, language analysis, etc.) they offer regular and timely conversation prompts, ask useful questions, and allow the client to figure out the answers by themselves. They can work in any language preferred by the client. Preliminary research shows that chatbots are as effective as a coach to support goal attainment through reminders, nudges, resources, etc. Indeed, significant evidence exist in healthcare research that these chatbots are useful to assist with cognitive behavioral interventions.

Support for the group coach's reflective practice

- processing the feedback of participants received during or after the session or processing multisource feedback. Generating curated reflective prompts and continuous learning suggestions
- giving AI generated feedback, based on a comparison between what the AI would have decided vs. what the group coach has decided (retrospectively) or is about to decide (in real time). Arguably, AI can analyze vast amounts of data faster than a human being, they can identify patterns more precisely. They are devoid of a human being mental state which generates resistance or countertransference. They are also likely to be more consistent because they are not influenced by bodily factors such as hunger, tiredness, etc.

Co-coaching tool

- curating of knowledge resources for the group coach in preparation of a session
- curating resources for the participants before, during or after a session (ex: question, visual, short video, song, quote, article, book, webinar, etc.) to increase engagement and creativity
- answer technical or tactical questions asked by participants during the session
- sending prompts group members who would like to continue exchanging ideas, ask questions or support each other between group sessions

Other uses

Predictive analytics based on the previous recorded behaviours of the group may help the group coach better manage group dynamics. More simply, in similarly with what is used in sports, AI enhanced videos could provide actionable feedback to the participants, and to the coach too! Further down the line, we can imagine the use of augmented reality to create more immersive experiences for the group and the coach.

Issues with the use of AI as a decision aid

However, any type of AI assisted task requires on-going data collection to increase its performance. It is unclear who owns the data generated by a conversation with a chatbot, which raises troubling questions about confidentiality and privacy. From my perspective, until we are clearer on ways to protect privacy and confidentiality of the personal data used to produce this technology, it's too soon to use them. As I mentioned earlier, we need a more diverse pool of programmers who have similar experiences to those who are going to use the tools.

Individual and group development

AI will not be self-aware until they possess a concept of self, in other words, until they experience human consciousness. Because AI is not conscious, it cannot not experience compassion: it is unable to provide caring and nurturing empathy. In addition, AI is still incapable of wisdom because it is yet to extrapolate from one context to the other. These deficiencies compromise the ability of AI to build vertical cohesion with the group of members.

There is, however, an intriguing exception. In dyadic coaching, AI is starting to provide cognitive empathy, meaning the ability to accurately detect the emotional state of the client based on their body language and choice of words. This might be enough to provide a sense of a strong working alliance for the client (working alliance being defined as the combination of bonding and agreement between the client and the coach). Arguably, research convincingly shows that it is the perception of the strength of the working alliance by the client that mediates the success of coaching, not the level of working alliance experienced by the coach. If the AI provides consistent skills, in a well-meaning manner, according to agreed-upon principles, it is likely that the client will perceive a strong working alliance. In cognitive-behavioral therapy, some clients report feeling more safety and trust when they work with AI, which allows them to share more than they would if they worked with a human being. As a result, they experience better outcomes.

Reflective questions about Chapter 6

- How did you acquire your skills as a group coach?
- If you are considering adding group coaching to your practice, what is your plan to become a skilled practitioner?
- What aspects of the capacity model resonate for you?
- How do you engage in self-reflective practice? What benefits do you receive from it?
- If you participated in a job analyse process to create the competency model of the group coach, what would you add to the list I suggested in Table 6.1?
- What is your perspective on AI? Have you experimented with it?

Bibliography

Brown, S. W., & Grant, A. M. (2010). From GROW to GROUP: Theoretical issues and a practical model for group coaching in organisations. *Coaching: An International Journal of Theory, Research and Practice, 3*(1), 30–45.

Carroll, M., & Shaw, E. (2013). *Ethical maturity in the helping professions: Making difficult life and work decisions.* Jessica Kingsley Publishers.

Christian, B. (2020). *The alignment problem: Machine learning and human values.* W.W. Norton & Company.

Cserti, R. (2019). Essential facilitation skills for an effective facilitator. *Delivery Matters.*

Fumoto, E. (2016). Developing a group coaching model to cultivate creative confidence. *International Journal of Evidence Based Coaching & Mentoring.*

Gannon, J. M. (2021). Applying the lens of social movements to coaching and mentoring. *Philosophy of Coaching: An International Journal, 6*(1), 5–29.

Graßmann, C., & Schermuly, C. C. (2021). Coaching with artificial intelligence: Concepts and capabilities. *Human Resource Development Review, 20*(1), 106–126.

Gyllensten, K., Henschel, C., & Jones, G. (2020). The experience of executive group coaching–A qualitative study. *International Coaching Psychology Review, 15*(1), 37–43.

Hougaard, R., Carter, J., & Stembridge, R. (2024). The best leaders can't be replaced by AI. https://hbsp.harvard.edu/product/H07Z39-PDF-ENG

Kets de Vries, M. F. (2014). The group coaching conundrum. *International Journal of Evidence Based Coaching and Mentoring, 12*(1), 79–91.

Knight, C. (2017). The mutual aid model of group supervision. *The Clinical Supervisor, 36*(2), 259–281.

Mazzolini, M., & Maddison, S. (2003). Sage, guide or ghost? The effect of instructor intervention on student participation in online discussion forums. *Computers & Education, 40*(3), 237–253.

Passmore, J., & Woodward, W. (2023). Coaching education: Wake up to the new digital and AI coaching revolution! *International Coaching Psychology Review, 18*(1), 58–72.

Seiler, H. (2021). *Ebook: Using client feedback in executive coaching: Improving reflective practice* (4th edition). McGraw-Hill Education (UK).

Tasca, G. A. (2021). Twenty-five years of Group Dynamics: Theory, research and practice: Introduction to the special issue. *Group Dynamics: Theory, Research, and Practice, 25*(3), 205.

Terblanche, N. (2020). A design framework to create Artificial Intelligence Coaches. *International Journal of Evidence Based Coaching & Mentoring, 18*(2).

Thomas, G. J. (2005). Dimensions of facilitator education. *The IAF handbook of group facilitation: Best practices from the leading organisation in facilitation,* 525–541.

Thornton, C. (2010). *Group and team coaching: The essential guide.* Routledge.

Van der Veen, N., & Reid, A. (2021). *Amplifying personal and leadership development through group coaching.* Gordon Institute of Business Science. University of Pretoria.

Parting Words

I hope this book has delivered its promise to inspire you to expand the offering of group coaching to women leaders. Writing this book has been a fulfilling journey for me, allowing me to rediscover how group coaching is done and what benefits it can bring. I am thankful for the voices of researchers, group members, fellow practitioners, and futurists that have nourished me along the way.

Kruppaz, a Proto-Germanic word which means rounded mass, is at the origin of the word group. It is a perfect fit for the women leaders in my group who consistently excel at bonding, collaborating, and supporting each other. The Hungarian word *kocsi*, which means carriage, is at the origin of the word coach. As a group coach we provide the safe vehicle to transport these women leaders where they want to go. Notably, we provide a space for conversations, which comes from two Latin roots: *con*, which means with and *versare*, which means to turn.

There is still a lot of work to be done to professionalize group coaching. Research and theorization are still emergent, there is no credentialing process, and it is still not considered as a core leadership development intervention to ensure that gender balance and inclusion is achieved in organizations. I hope this book has achieved its objective to encourage more demand, more studies, more experimentation, and more initiatives to offer group coaching to women leaders.

As I close this journey, I am thinking about the future women leaders and the different challenges they might have to face. The 9th Women in the Workplace study (McKinsey, 2008–2023) indicates a slower increase of gender diversity from entry level to Director level. At the same time, research indicates that younger generations hold different views about what a fulfilling career looks like. They aspire to more flexible days, hybrid workplaces, and career breaks to balance their personal and professional lives. There continues to be a tendency to promote women based on what they have done in the past, while promoting men for their potential. In addition, over the last decade, the unattainable concept of ideal parenting has surfaced, which

DOI: 10.4324/9781003465195-8

pressures working women (and some willing working men) to spend more time and resources raising their children than the previous generations of women did. In this context, I see a potential to use group coaching as a safe space for future women leaders to support each other as they navigate these new norms.

In addition, calling on my pragmatic perspective, I see real potential for group coaching men leaders. Group coaching might encourage them to deploy strengths that they have repressed such as collaboration, transparency, empathy, or service orientation, because they have been labelled as feminine. Arguably, these strengths will be necessary to respond to the external forces that are increasingly shaping their professional and personal lives, including constant disruptions, constant changes, artificial intelligence, global complexity, and volatility, to name a few. These strengths will also likely enhance their gender inclusiveness. In that respect, I see group coaching for male leaders as one of the conduits for building stronger, gender balanced, leadership teams. And, who knows, men might also be inspired to let go of the ideal worker myth and start giving themselves permission to balance their nurturer and provider roles.

Connecticut, USA, March 2024.

Bibliography

Chamorro-Premuzic, T., & Gallop, C. (2020). Leadership lessons men can learn from women. *Harvard Business Review*, *1*.

Taylor & Francis (2021). Manuscript writing and formatting guide. Taylor & Francis. https://www.routledge.com/our-customers/authors/publishing-guidelines

Young, G. (2022). Women, naturally the best leaders for the 21st century? In *Transpersonal Leadership in Action* (pp. 82–94). Routledge.

Index

Pages in *italics* refer to figures and pages in **bold** refer to tables.

Printed in the United States
by Baker & Taylor Publisher Services